around the bend (again)

twisted ramblings of
motorcycle columnist max burns

a selection from
the final two millennia

Astorville, Ontario, Canada

This book is a collection of columns written by the author, the columns originally published in *Cycle Canada* magazine under the column title *Around the Bend*. Each column is a reflection of the author's mood at the time of writing, and may not relate to how the author feels about any given topic today. Or tomorrow. But we're not sure about the following day. The stories and comments are being published for entertainment purposes only. If you are not entertained, stop reading.

© Copyright 2003 by Max Burns

All rights reserved. No part of this book—or the author for that matter—may be reproduced or transmitted in any form or by any means, electronic or mechanical, including photocopying, recording, or by any information storage and retrieval system, without prior written permission of the publisher or the author's dog, Martha.

Cataloguing in Publication Data

Burns, Max, 1948–
Around the Bend (again), a selection from the final two millennia

ISBN 0-9730263-1-6
1. Burns I. Title. 1. Motorcyling–Anecdotes. 2. Motorcycles–Anecdotes.
GV1059.5.B87 2003   629.28'475   C2003-903446-1

Published by
Word Dust Press, RR 1, Astorville, ON P0H 1B0

Printed and bound in Canada by Friesens, Altona, MB R0G 0B0
Photography by Max Burns, Hugh McLean, and Jackie Quinton
Layout and artwork by Word Dust Press

Contents

The ultimate reason to ride   1

The premise   2

Foreword ho   5

The Selection

How to write off a bike, without even working at it   9
Seeing the world without taxing the odometer   12
In search of Utopia and the universal balance   15
A simple wave isn't simple anymore   18
Bench racing with a side order of fries   21
I can see farther when the leaves are gone   24
Adding to the confusion, just for fun   27
Mass transit isn't healthy for people and other living things   30
On the gas and sideways, sliding to infinity   33
Boneheads, meatheads and pig-headed bicycloids   36
Tales from the Agent Orange Death Wagon   39
A nutcase on the road to Showcase delirium   42
Throwing our helmets into the political fray   45
Gamesmanship and the traffic stream   48

Spruce trees and speed limits owe it all to saps	51
A collector of rare and unusual taste	54
Excerpts from the notes of a dazed traveller: Part I	57
Excerpts from the notes of a dazed traveller: Part 11	60
Singular qualities of dual-purpose motorcycles	63
In search of the ultimate garage sale, sort of	66
Thanks for the free ride, we needed that	69
Measuring up to memory	72
Scratch for dough, deep-fried	75
Avoid risk at your peril	78
Upload this, sunshine	81
Your ticket to their profits	84
You go this way, I'll go that way	87
Escape goats and other excuses	90
Here's a prize for you	93
One-upmanship for two	96
Mandatory and predatory	99
Just try to wiggle out of this	102
Bituminous bump and grind	105
Passion versus utility	108
The end is nigh. Maybe	111
Safe at any speed	114
Middle-finger discount	117
Unsafe at home	120
Pretty new, but not too pretty	123
Not in the forecast	126
Put the best to rest	129
Reason and prudence	132
Been there, bought the T-shirt	135

Make plans to improvise	138
Running on emptiness	141
The atlas unshrugged	144
Does it hurt to smile?	147
On the road again	150
Go fast, save the Earth	153
It's just a bike	156
Let me make two points	159
How stupid of me	162
Running on mountain time	165
Benchmark perspective	168
The great unravelling	171
Beemer me up	174
Who's the poseur?	177
Safe underwear at any speed	180
Sidecar à la carte	183
Book Order Form	last page, eh?

The ultimate reason to ride

by Pablo Taylor

December 18, 2000

From blacksmith to wordsmith, a crudely penned ode,
To a man in search of the ultimate road,
Sweepers and esses and right-angle bends
As long as there's asphalt the quest never ends.
There'll be dust-clouds and washboard and gravel, by heck,
But just try to follow Max on his lifelong trek
And you'll notice that swirling around in his wake
Are pie crusts, whipped cream, and pieces of cake.
The "ultimate road"? Maybe I was hasty,
Max is in search of the ultimate pastry!

© Copyright 2000 by Pablo Taylor

Poem courtesy of Pablo: poet, blacksmith, Triumph whisperer, and proprietor of Strawberry Fields Ironworks. Strawberry Fields is a "not much profit" organization dedicated to ingenuity, artistry, and original designs. It can be found on Hwy 522, just east of Arnstein, Ontario, Canada.

The Premise

Sometime 2003

I am a privileged and spoiled writer. For the most part, I write about what I want, when I want, a philosophy that has endowed me with a reputation for turning down at least as many assignments as I accept. True, this is not the best route to riches, but hey, if wealth was a prime motivator I sure as heck wouldn't have chosen writing as a career. Come to think of it, I didn't really choose it, I sort of eased into it. Ostensibly, I was looking for a way to avoid a real job. Subconsciously, I was looking for a means of expression, an avenue to get some ideas out for discussion, a public platform for a few of my jokes. Although my words subsequently travelled down several literary paths, such as off-the-grid water and sewage systems, the quest for food nirvana, noise pollution, architecture, travel, docks, repairing lawn mowers, fireplaces, and on and on, being a Canadian with an interest in motorcycles countersteered me to *Cycle Canada* magazine right from the beginning. So the relationship began, one that would see me operating in a variety of capacities for the magazine, most notably as author of *Around the Bend*.

Writing a regular column is a neat gig, particularly when the mandate is to be witty and controversial, with at least some tenuous link to a passion such as motorcycling. *Around the Bend* became my personal soapbox, a place to rant and rave about perceived injustices, to mock the establishment, to poke fun at everything and everyone (especially me), to explore life and its absurdities, and to offer my impressions on bikes

(to the chagrin of some manufacturers), people (to the chagrin of some people), and places (to the chagrin of some residents), always with that link to motorcycles.

Truth is, linking a topic to motorcycles isn't difficult because motorcyclists are such a wonderfully diverse group of people, in philosophy, disposition, and career choices. The challenge is to maintain the surprise element in a column that appears in every issue of the magazine. The reader shouldn't know what to expect other than a good read. I don't mind irritating a reader–in fact I don't even mind if a reader stops being a reader out of anger over my words. What I don't want is to lose a reader because of boredom. There are writers who do very well churning out the same old crap, column after column, story after story, for undoubtedly there is comfort in uniformity. But I don't want my readers to be comfortable. I want my readers to be entertained with serendipity, to have emotions stirred, to think. Doesn't work every time, or for everyone, but that still remains the goal.

Which explains why I quit writing *Around the Bend* at the end of 1989. My head-space was in a bit of turmoil at the time and I feared this distraction might put that goal at risk, that I might begin writing the column out of obligation rather than pleasure. So I killed it. Fortunately, Chris Knowles filled the page in *Cycle Canada* with a new column, *Off Camber*. Fortunately again (at least for me), seven years later he too experienced a similar sense of approaching burn-out and retired his column. When *Cycle Canada* asked if I would like to resurrect *Around the Bend*, I quickly agreed. I was ready. My desire to write the column had reignited. And it continues to burn as I tap these words into my trusty, old 386 IBM-clone.

Another nifty aspect to writing a regular column that I hadn't anticipated way back in the 1980s is the relationship that evolves between writer and reader. Some of you actually believe what I say. I mean, I usually believe it too, but the degree to which my words occasionally hit home with the readers can be very flattering and very rewarding. Even humbling at times. So I never lose sight of my obligation to you to provide honest journalism. And sometimes my words fall into a reader's life just at the right time and in the right manner to sum up an important moment for that person. When that happens, there is nothing more gratifying for me as a writer.

And therein lies the premise for this book–a bit of self-indulgence for the both of us. I wanted *Around the Bend* readers to tell me about their most memorable columns, both favourites and the ones that pissed them off. To my surprise, the most frequent response to this request was "I liked them all," which was nice, but not a big help, guys. Hell, I don't even like them all. So I sifted through the many responses, tossed in a few of my own faves, and *voilà*, a book is born. The columns appear as published in *Cycle Canada*, by date, along with a few of the readers' comments and/or author's excuses. Enjoy the read (again).

Thanks
An author's thanks always risk being a tedious read, but there are a few folks in particular who should be singled out, so here goes.

Thanks to the two editors of *Cycle Canada* who presided during the period covered in this book, both of whom tolerated—and even encouraged—my eccentricities; John Cooper, there when I began writing for the magazine, and Bruce Reeve, who became editor in 1989. And thanks too for Bruce Reeve's cooperation and editorial assistance in producing this retrospect of *Around the Bend*.

Thanks to Hugh McLean who did a wonderful job of making me look my best for the column photo, and for permission to re-use that complimentary image on the back cover of this book.

Thanks to Pablo for permission to use his poetic revelation of my true motives for riding.

Thanks to Jackie for her years of perseverance and participation in my unconventional life. Bit soppy perhaps, but she has certainly earned the thanks.

And thanks to you, the reader. It's been great to lead so many of you *Around the Bend*.

Foreword Ho
by Bruce Reeve
(editor of Cycle Canada magazine, 1989-)

Some other time 2003

I used to think it strange that nobody ever asked me, "What is Max Burns really like?" It wasn't that nobody was interested; the opposite was true. What struck me as odd was that readers of Cycle Canada magazine would try to tell me what Max Burns was like, because so many of them felt they knew him from his writing. Well, some of these readers may have been simply delusional, but this powerful connection between Max and his readers is one of the secrets of his success. I've talked to other magazine editors who have noted the same reaction to Max's work. Readers respond to it. Frankly, we're mystified. But as Max would tell you, ours is not to reason why. We should just print his stuff and send him the cheques. Of course, being an editor, I can't simply leave it at that.

On one level, the reason Max's writing appeals to so many people is that he seems an open, genuine and unpretentious soul, a devoted father and husband, sometimes even sweetly sentimental. Then there's the other Max—deliberately perverse, anarchistic, joyously rude and bitterly misanthropic. But then don't we all feel that way sometimes?

Although I've known Max for many years now, there remains an air of mystery about him. He's a consummate pro as a writer, with a sheaf of national magazine awards to his credit, but he's never lost the boyish impulse to write something nasty on the wall. Although Max has evolved as a wordsmith during the time I've known him, he seemed to spring out of nowhere with most of his style and writing character fully formed. I've wondered, at times, if Max isn't in some sort of witness protection program–from some other solar system. His writing can flow with grace and power, yet on rare occasions produce the strangest spelling and grammar mistakes I've ever seen, of the sort you wouldn't expect from someone whose first language is English–or from someone born in this galaxy.

Max would be the first to tell you he is not entirely comfortable on our planet. He speaks with horror of a four-year period in his distant past when he held a lucrative full-time job, something to do with bookkeeping apparently, following a wanton education as an art student. There are a number of unexplained gaps on Max's resume, which will probably forever bar him from a management-trainee position at Burger King (though few are so adept at flipping whoppers...).

Fortunately for us, Max chose to invent a life for himself as a writer, starting as a contributor to Cycle Canada. Within a few years he was assigned his own column space, though he also continued to write feature stories. For a brief period in the late '80s, Max worked next to me as an editor in our office, but this seemed to revive memories of his previous full-time job, and he soon fled Toronto back to northern Ontario and the freedom of freelancing.

You'll notice that Max's Around the Bend columns ceased for around seven years before resuming in 1998. He continued to contribute feature stories to Cycle Canada during some of this time, and on one occasion was assigned to cover a lavish, if poorly organized, trip to Italy to survey the operations of Ducati, sampling some production, prototype and race bikes in the process. I later heard that the Ducati people didn't quite know what to make of Max. They found him a bit strange. Maybe so, but Max rode the wheels off a fleet of Ducatis and brought back a story both hilarious and insightful; nobody among the U.S. press on the same trip wrote anything half as good.

Around the same time Max's freelance career began to flourish as a writer for Harrowsmith and particularly Cottage Life magazine, where he won numerous awards. During this same period he went back to the land with his patient and beautiful wife Jackie, first living in a shack on the edge of wilderness while building an innovative, environmentally friendly home set in a hillside.

Having chosen to earn a living as freelance writer, Max has turned to such practical subjects as dock building, water systems and outhouses for articles and books that help pay the bills. Apparently he's even been contracted by the Egyptian government to help draw up standards for dock construction on the Red Sea coast. God help them. But that's business. What's really fun for Max is writing about whatever he damn well pleases. In the past this has even included science fiction and romance novels, which remain stuffed in a drawer somewhere, but writing a column on motorcycling for Cycle Canada has allowed him to run freely with his imagination while still earning a few bucks in the process. It's been a great process, really–Max writes Around the Bend for his own amusement, and we read it for ours.

Many of the columns collected here may be familiar to Max's long-time readers, but I found them fun to read again and expect you will too. For those encountering Around the Bend for the first time, all I can say is this: the road is twisted, and you're in for a treat.

MAX BURNS

How to write off a bike, without even working at it

August 1985

I never used to worry much about dropping my bike. Blind corners covered in sand and gravel, rain sliding off an oil-soaked surface of new asphalt, black ice lurking in the shadows of extended seasons—all inconveniences to be sure, but drop my bike? You must be kidding.

Don't get me wrong. I have always worn a helmet and been into leather (hold the whips), knowing full well that the possibility of a crash is very real. But. Before it was always the other guy I distrusted—the non-attentive pilot of that family station wagon waiting to turn left into my path, or whatever. The single-bike accident where I pick up the tab after picking up my bike was not a serious consideration.

My first Around the Bend column, chosen by my wife, Jackie, not because of any intrinsic merit but simply because she thought the book should start with number one. Good news is, my writing improved over time. Bad news is, motorcycle repair costs have got worse.
—Max

Now, I worry a little.

It started last year when I purchased one of Japan's latest Flash Gordon retro-rockets. This bike corners, stops, steers and accelerates better than anything else I have ever ridden. My ability to avoid potential disaster has correspondingly increased. So too, has my confidence. Yet still, I worry.

It's the costs that have done it. Not the purchase price of the machine—that only made my banker worry. Besides, my new car figured in at more than twice what the bike did, and I drive that with wild abandon and scarcely a care. It is the cost of motorcycle repairs that has me scared. Motorcycle accident repairs. I would really have to prang the car up badly before it would be considered a write-off, or even a gross, major expense. But the bike?

Not long ago, a month-old Interceptor I know of was written off. The frame was good, engine okay, fork straight, wheels and tires fine, the damage being almost exclusively cosmetic. Yet the cost of replacing the trashed pieces, never mind the labour, exceeded the value of the bike!

You want more?

A GPz crawling to a stop is schmucked in the rear by a small-calibre bike travelling at about 8 km/h. The GPz goes down, sustaining only superficial damage. Cost of parts—about $700. This scares me.

If my beloved two-wheeled treasure were to touch pavement with anything but its tires, I likely would need a fifth mortgage on the homestead in order to finance its restoration.

And I'm not just talking about accidents involving vehicles in motion. Even a bike toppling at a standstill can ruin a healthy bank account. An acquaintance recently discovered his superbike resting horizontally in a parking lot. Not a pretty sight. The repair bill for that seemingly minor fall rose to more than $600. Now that's downright ugly.

Clearly, the responsibility for this disgrace lies with the manufacturers. They are the source of this high-priced fragility, both from the standpoint of design and replacement costs. And they are the ones who must act, and now, for the sake of their continued growth and motorcycling in general. Motorcycling must be made to be more crashworthy.

I am not suggesting some Nader-inspired, energy-absorbing touch-bumper system to facilitate the safe execution of random 5 mph lunges into things hard, but surely the situation can be improved upon. Simple things, like snap-off mirrors, and strong engine guards tastefully incorporated into the overall design. Finishes with better scratch resistance might be too much to hope for. How about standardized headlights? And in the category of avoiding the problem in the first place, mirrors that reflect more than rider elbows would be a godsend (the unwillingness to provide this basic right is a classic example of paying lip service to safety to benefit the showroom priorities of fashion).

As for the high cost of replacing battlescarred bits, that is a real and long-standing problem. Do not look for a solution as long as manufacturers and distributors must continue to stock the huge inventories of non-interchangeable parts necessitated by self-imposed heterogeneous product design. Current prices might not seem so out of line, however, if the goods supplied were not so prone to destruct upon impact.

What will it take to motivate manufacturers to push away from the cash registers a moment and instigate changes? Good, far-sighted vision, I hope, for failure to do so can only lead to powerful lobby groups pounding on government doors. Groups like the insurance industry, who will point, quite justifiably, to high damage claims. Groups like the self-righteous consumer advocates who rise up in their K-Mart suits and base-line four-door bandwagons to protest whenever it looks as if somebody might be having a little fun. And of course, that ever-present troupe of whiplash lawyers with the fire of mega-buck lawsuits burning in their eyes. It would be ruinous.

We've seen it happen with cars. The automotive industry learned to regret its ostrich-like attitude, while auto enthusiasts suffered. I fear the same action of blind ignorance that suffocated automobile technology in the '70s is close upon us, brought on by an industry's indifference and narrow-minded fiscal priorities. That action is called government intervention.

Now that worries me.

Seeing the world without taxing the odometer

December 1985

It is possible to cross a continent without touring. I have done so myself. It happens when expediency supersedes exploration and a destination point becomes the only point of the journey. The vehicle may be very conducive to touring, yet is transformed into mere transportation by the singular quest for kilometres rolling over on odometers. The pressing need to complete the trip pushes aside the real and potential gains of getting absorbed in the land.

Touring is a state of mind, not an odometer reading. It is the difference between passing through and being there; the difference between shadowy glimpses and vivid memories. To judge a tour by the mileage is like judging success by the bank

Touring to experience an area rather than to quickly pass through it is one of several reoccurring Around the Bend themes. This was my first shot at it, and the first column to really strike a chord with Cycle Canada readers, judging from the responses received at the time.
—Max

account—it's a convenient yardstick for those who missed the objective.

To tour is not merely to arrive, but to ease into the surroundings in search of intrinsic character and charms. It means getting off the bike now and then to touch the land. Chat with the locals. Get a feeling for the country. How does it sit with the senses? This can't be accomplished by mere "How's the weather been?" encounters with gas-pump jockeys every 200 km or so. It necessitates a slower pace, bringing the beat of the engine down closer to the pulse, giving the mind time to relax and think about things other than crazy traffic and rushing stop signs.

The places I have the best memories of are the ones where I took the occasional recess from riding to capture a small sample of the world. I think of those kids I met in the outback of Newfoundland who were dazzled by an Aspencade's digital wonderland, and whose resultant verbal outburst I could not make head nor tail of. Or the privately run museum of miscellaneous bits of clanking machinery and steam-powered junk on the south shore of the St. Lawrence, where once again, my inability to comprehend the local language proved no barrier to a good time and friendly rapport with the natives. Or the rancher in Alberta who was a dead-ringer for Clint Eastwood; a forgotten restaurant in small-town Ontario trapped in a late-'40s time warp (owner included); and a gypsy retired couple on Vancouver Island who assured me that someday I would be able to afford a huge motorhome like theirs and wouldn't have to suffer the meagre ways of my current means of travel. None of this would have existed had I not chosen to be there instead of simply passing through.

It takes time to go the distance and even more time to stop. If the days are in short supply, don't be tempted to increase the speed, just shorten the distance. It isn't necessary to travel far. There is a point at which a hurried long haul can tumble over that fine line of excess, resembling more an endurance race than a tour. Speed is certainly no bad thing in itself, but is it still possible to make contact with the space through which one is passing when all is a blur?

The places I like the least are usually the ones I simply buzzed through and didn't take time to discover. Saskatchewan, for instance. Can't stand it. No matter which end of the country I approach it from, it still constitutes too much prairie. Alberta and Manitoba, they've got enough of the stuff to cause a mild ripple of interest. Saskatchewan is just plain overkill (sorry about the pun).

However, much as it pains me to admit this in print, I think my impression of the province could be a false reading, taken as it was from the edges of the Trans-Canada Highway. Speed readers always miss something. They know the story, but did they get the feeling? The next trip out West, I intend to slow down, and read between the lines.

Shame the place is so godawful flat, though.

A closer look doesn't always guarantee a favourable review. Some places just don't stand up well to close scrutiny. A few years back, during an attack of uncharacteristic mass-transit adventurism, I abandoned my bike in the city of Cochrane and took the Polar Bear Express north to Moosonee. This town, and its famed rail ride, are best experienced via the pages of government travel-guide hyperbole while coddled in the living-room armchair sipping on tour dreams. Any attempt at honest evaluation that I could sneak past the editors of this magazine would be far too charitable, so let's just call it a disappointment and leave it at that. That's the chance you take with touring.

But if the pace is right, more often than not the place is also right. And even if it rains the whole trip, as it has on every occasion I have visited Canada's eastern seaboard, I still come back feeling better for the experience. I may bitch a lot at the time, but always in retrospect, I know it was worthwhile. Fun even.

In the final analysis, a tour should have a greater impact upon the participants than the odometer. The hasty traversing of great expanses certainly has its own rewards and purpose, but having the opportunity to just be there is not one of them. I like a tour that leads me inward, into the land and into myself, because, more than a form of travel, touring is a state of mind.

Note: My judgment of Saskatchewan was to change radically when, years later, I followed my own advice as put forth in this column. Turns out, it's southern Manitoba that's so bloody flat. Yet even that bit of over-stretched topography makes for a grand place to tour if viewed from the right head-space.
—Max

In search of Utopia and the universal balance

March 1986

For centuries, this elusive goal has captivated the thoughts of man. Skeptics refer to it as bunk, a figment of overactive imaginations. Ken Rosevear knows it exists. As a matter of fact, he lives there. RR2 Utopia.

Now before you get all excited and start loading up the old RD with worldly possessions, family dog, and a few extra quarts of two-stroke oil, let me fill you in on something. Utopia isn't on the map. It's stashed away at the end of a dead-end county road, asleep roughly half-way between a military camp and Bustop, mid-Ontario. And it looks just like a hundred other quiet residential areas in the country.

What brought me to Utopia was Rosevear Motorcycle Works, Ken's effort at avoiding a regular job.

For me, this one set the standard for all subsequent Around the Bend columns. Its approach was fresh and fun, connecting a few of the disorganized dots between motorcycles, motorcyclists, and the rest of the universe. And I had a good time writing it, which invariably shows.
—Max

He used to have one of those (a regular job) when he worked for Can-Am back in the days when they built a Canadian motorcycle. Now, he rebuilds vintage motorcycles; mostly old British stuff. Utopia seems a likely place to carry on such a fanciful endeavour.

Of course, it was not a mere whim or fancy that inspired my trip there. Cold, analytical logic lay behind each knock upon his door. I needed a dose of old British stuff. No, I haven't gone completely off my rocker. Not yet. I still don't own anything Italian. Where the logic comes in (you've been waiting for this, right?) is that I had to have a balance. All things in life must balance.

When millions are starving in far away lands, I eat more here in Canada. When millions here in Canada wanted a job, I quit mine. The universal balance. I call it my theory of cosmic equilibrium.

All Ken had for sale at the time was a fairly clean Triumph TRW, which he graciously allowed me to take for a ride. I stepped on the brake when I wanted to shift, and made rude noises with the gearbox when I wanted to stop.

Reluctantly, but mercifully, I ended the bump and grind review. The Triumph was neat, but a little… oh, I guess dull is the word. I wanted something special. After all, this was Utopia.

No problem, says Ken, and off we roared into Suburban Utopia to look at some other bikes. We checked out a Norton Commando. Ken spotted all sorts of irregularities, including the fact that the serial numbers didn't match up. And we dropped in to see Brian Van Biglongdutchname.

At first glance, Brian's 1955 BSA A7 Shooting Star didn't really turn my crank. Probably the colour. It's kind of an insipid, polychromatic green. Original, they tell me. Yawn. But when Brian went to fire it up, my interest warmed.

No choke. The operator has to "tickle" the shared float bowl of the twin carbs, dousing his hand and sundry BSA bits in gasoline. Great! A fire hazard. Down goes the kickstarter and oh my gawd, what a splendid cacophony of anti-social sounds—the barely restrained charge of a British twin. Rule Britannia! You could almost hear the oil leaking. I knew I had my balance.

Balance to what, you ask? Well, over the past year or so, I've been increasingly busy pounding my little pinkies to their stumps on ye olde Olivetti. (Okay, put the hankies away. This is no time for petty sarcasm.) My friends said "Get a word processor!" I said "Get lost! No computer shall dwell within the sanctity of my house!"

This is not the emotional cry of some crazed reactionary. Objective reasoning lies behind this outburst. I am philosophically opposed to any instrument of mankind capable of playing Donkey Kong. Besides, anything the great washed masses judge to be mandatory I usually do my best to avoid.

However, begrudgingly, deep down inside I knew that, sooner or later, I would have to give in, if only for the sake of my abused fingers. So I bought the BSA. Just after I bought the computer.

Upon my arrival back home, my son zipped the boxes of electronic wizardry into the house. He understands things computer. (The offspring always turn against you.)

Meanwhile, I unloaded the BSA and tried to start it up for an interested neighbour ("I used to own one of those, except mine had a...").

I tickled it and coaxed it and threatened it and made a lot of noise cursing it, but my Shooting Star refused to light up the silence of the night. Then the kickstarter jammed.

I rolled the lame beast into the garage, parked it, and went inside to play with the computer. Cosmic equilibrium.

The next morning, I solved the problem of the kickstarter and fired up the Beezer, riding it up and down the driveway as various friends dropped over to witness my latest madness. Reports from the house claimed the windows shook. Tremors from a Shooting Star, I retorted.

Ken Rosevear knew it all along. Now I do too. Utopia does exist.

That afternoon, I sat down in front of the computer to create my first silicon-aided masterpiece. The printer jammed.

At least the universal balance was now tilted in my favour.

A simple wave isn't simple anymore

April 1986

Years ago, enthusiasts on wheels always waved to each other. Bikers would wave "how-do" to any fellow biker, hot-rodders waved to hot-rodders, and sports car freaks waved to those in other sports cars.

Now, people don't seem to be so liberal with their "how-dos."

This heavy insight came to me while enduring the pleasures of an inter-city bus, that transportation equivalent to purgatory. It's an ideal place for deep thought, because you can leave it on the seat with the candy wrappers when you disembark. So there I sat—express, non-smoking please—pondering the cause and significance of the lost wave.

The world of vehicular enthusiasm has experienced some drastic change over the past 20 years.

The act of waving to a fellow motorcyclist in passing is akin to a religious ceremony—some do it, some don't, some wave only to specific riders riding specific brands of motorcycles, but all fervently believe in the righteousness of their actions. Since writing this column I have changed my mind regarding the importance of the wave, but time occasionally does that sort of thing to you, doesn't it? So wave if it makes you feel good.

—Max

Take the hot-rod, if you can find one, a vehicle of proud homebrew ingenuity largely superseded by the 20-grand, air-conditioned Transamacon; an owner's involvement now regulated to making monthly payments, or perhaps choosing between the velour or vinyl seat coverings. And what about sports cars? With the exception of a few mega-dollar wonders, they have become the endangered automotive species of the '80s. So who is left to carry the wave?

Bikers. There are more around now than ever. Yet have they not been smitten by the specialization bugaboo? "Don't wave at them son, those aren't our kind." Waves are budgeted, spent for the most part only when touring out on the open road, each faction adhering to strict rules of technique.

The so-called "touring crowd" (those with very large bikes and hard luggage) sit up straight and throw out a big wave to each other in passing. Picture the Lone Ranger leaving town on a Gold Wing.

Sportbike riders, because of their mandatory go-fast crouch, generally restrict their semaphore antics to the lifting of two fingers from the left handgrip, though, with the racer fairing becoming more prevalent (and therefore obscuring this manoeuvre), we are beginning to see the left arm shoot out and down to about knee level, then held. Picture the Lone Ranger leaving town with a dislocated shoulder.

Those riding cruiser bikes just nod to each other. It's a subtle thing; you have to watch for it, which is probably why most cruiserists insist on open-face helmets. Picture the Queen riding a Virago as she acknowledges the adulation of her subjects lining the parade route.

Of course, all these rules get thrown to the wind when it's raining. When the whole world is wet, and two bikers approach through the spray, no matter what they are riding, a dripping, soggy leather glove is invariably raised in greeting. Picture two daredevils who, while floating down the Niagara River, come to realize they are about to go over the falls at the same time. There is an understanding, an appreciation of what the other is going through, like comrades in shared suffering.

Hold everything, we may be on to something, Jack! Is it not that same sense of shared suffering that bonded together the passing souls of waves gone by? Hot-rodders knew the sacrifices necessary to get that machine coming at them simply... coming at them, so they saluted each other out of respect. Sports car owners were only too aware of the time spent with head under hood in order to bask in a patch of sunny driving weather.

And we've all heard the almost biblical tales of having to work on a bike for six days so it could be ridden on the seventh. Every rider waved, regardless of what they were on. Even Harley riders waved! (I don't know what they do now. I know they don't wave to me on British or Japanese bikes. I'll ask a couple of friends and get back to you.)

Without intending to cast judgment, let me point out that, good or bad, it took more than money to be an enthusiast prior to the '80s. Each machine was the owner's, 100 percent, either because of the modifications he had made to it, or by the very fact that it was running. In both cases, the results came from owner involvement.

Today, it is possible for anyone with money to own an enthusiast's vehicle. You don't have to be a mechanic anymore, which, I suppose, is good. But don't expect to get waved at much. Even Corvette owners don't wave like they used to, but this is likely due to the latest models being so expensive only lawyers can afford them, and they aren't disposed to befriend anyone unless there's a buck in it.

Fortunately, however, all this philosophical rambling leads to an upbeat finish. For old-wave fans, there is one close-knit group who are still at it, come rain or shine, waving to their comrades, regardless of which make or model they pilot. I am refering, of course, to inter-city bus drivers. And all you need is a coach seat to somewhere in order to be part of the action.

Not that I'd recommend it over any contemporary enthusiast's machine, mind you, but it is comforting to know some folks are still suffering.

Bench racing with a side order of fries

October 1986

Nineteen eighty-six is going to go down as a bad year for motorcycling—bike prices are way up, insurance premiums have risen to ridiculous, dealers are struggling for survival, and Lee Roy's didn't put out its picnic table.

Lee Roy's is one of the fast food emporiums on Lakeshore Drive. Without question, this northern epicurean exclusive features some of the best burgers and fries known to man. But what really sets Lee Roy's apart from the others, or at least what used to, is that picnic table. Picture the typical scene a mere 12 months ago.

Saturday night with nothing to do? Motor on up to Lee Roy's, order a mess of fries, squeeze out a spot at the table, and enjoy the show.

I've always strived to bring the reader along with me, to place the reader right in the midst of whatever it is I'm describing. I want the reader to feel, smell, hear, taste, and see everything I do. Obviously, this doesn't mean the reader will come to the same conclusions (thankfully, for the rest of the world), but at least we have shared similar inputs. This is not an easy goal to achieve consistently but extremely satisfying when it works. With this column, I felt it worked.

—Max

Although the city's designated Main Street has been gussied up in one of those ye olde interlocking brick efforts geared to "save the downtown core," eyesore Lakeshore is really where it's at—junk food alley, four lanes of crazy drivers, and enough space between stop lights to really get some noise up with an unbaffled header system. Lakeshore is Cruise Avenue on a Saturday night, and Lee Roy's picnic table makes for the best seat in the house, curbside centre.

You can hear them coming, full throttle off the lights. Four-into-ones blasting out the howls of hyper-tense four-stroke aggression. Two-strokes snarling through pregnant pea-shooters, screaming like Cuisinarts smoking into orbit. And as they approach, each machine revs high, restricted to the lower gears in order to extend the anti-social qualities of internal combustion.

Headlights jump through the traffic, leaping from tiny space to tiny space until they bob up even with our table. A rider looks over to verify that someone is watching. No sense performing before an empty house.

Ahead, the traffic stops. A car load of preppies is turning into the Plastic Arches across the road for a bite of something our creator would likely have trouble recognizing he ever had a hand in.

Suddenly, our star rider is confronted with a flock of mandatory third-brake lights flashing bright red before him. Panic overtakes his nervous system. Tires lock up, rubber howls, the bike slides, and *ho, look out!* I almost knocked the ketchup over. Sorry guys.

There's another good thing about the picnic table. You can bring out whole squirtzer bottles of ketchup and vinegar instead of having to fiddle with those damnable plastic packets that end up exploding all over everything except hamburgers or fries.

The sliding stops about a quarter-pounder away from disaster as the street-squirrel slinks off into the inside lane amid considerable loss of stature.

Now that's entertainment.

Naturally, all this excitement stirs up quite a thirst, so it's time for a chocolate shake, extra thick, save my spot at the table.

Here come some Harleys. Harley engines don't scream, they bark, mean and slow, like junkyard dogs. You can hear their pistons moving. Almost count each revolution. The riders? A genuine mystery. They always look so serious when they parade by, as if on a mission of extreme import, like heading to their mother's funeral. Which started 15 minutes ago.

I would have trouble being an official Harley rider. The bikes are just too much dog-gone fun to expect me, of all people, to maintain any sort of serious deportment for any serviceable length of time. How do those dudes do it, anyway?

One more thing. You can order your fries in various sized boxes, but we usually opt for the family pack. Of course, this can lead to a few problems because some like ketchup and vinegar and salt, while some don't. But it's cheaper to buy in bulk, so the table crowd learns to eat around the inconvenience of personal peculiarities.

Speaking of peculiarities, will you look at that! Quick, count the lights ...23, 24... rats, he's gone. If I owned a full-dresser, I think I'd purchase a few shares in a battery company to boot.

The space between passing bikes is filled with conversation about bikes. "Whaddaya think of that new GZ Thingamajig?" "Say, did you hear how well Whatzisname is doing at the track this year? He's cleaning up!"

And when the fries are all gone, we too clean up, then take our turn profiling along the Saturday night stage of Lakeshore Drive.

That was how things went last year. This year, the price of everything is up, the picnic table is gone, and we haven't been back to Lee Roy's. It just wouldn't be the same.

But. Have you heard the rumours for '87? The manufacturers are supposed to be bringing out some pretty nifty stuff. And Lee Roy's a new table. Which brings us to the good part about a bad year. Next year. With that new table, it has got to be a winner.

Note: Sadly, a few years after the writing of this column, Lee Roy's folded up and went to that great burger haven in the cosmic deep frier. I don't know what happened to its picnic table.
—Max

I can see farther when the leaves are gone

November 1986

Once the leaves are gone, a visual gap some three or four metres wide opens up between the houses behind mine to give me my post-summer view of the world. From my study, it is possible to watch the weather roll in across the lake from the islands. Water and weather tend to work together to feed a man's musings. Right now, the weather is grey and the water looks cold.

BRAAAAAA! There goes Paul on his XR350. On the road out front. I can tell it's him by the "geary" sound of the motor.

An XR350 on the street? When the Ontario government brought into force its ill-conceived rules of the off-road, Paul put a street plate on his dirt bike. He has even less patience for governmen-

This is another theme that tends to creep into my writing on a frequent basis, the idea that risk is an important facet of the human make-up, and that the person taking the risk should be accountable for the outcome. It's all about freedom, a once-sacred concept whose meaning has been usurped by politicians and "the system" (whatever the hell that is) for their own gains. This column also deals with my pal Paul, his inclusion always making for a fun story.

–Max

tal bureaucracy and legislative stupidity than I.

BRAAAAAA! There he goes again. A couple more times around the block, and the doorbell will ring. He usually does this without dismounting.

"Max! What's new?"

Through that narrow gap, my mind had just been looking at what was new—a nation no longer willing to accept the responsibilities for its own actions, a nation that was quickly learning to demand financial compensation for its own stupidity, dramatized sufferings (vicarious or otherwise), and exaggerated losses through outragious liability suits, all encouraged to extremes by the greed of parasitic lawyers who in turn were encouraged by judges and politicians who in turn were lawyers themselves. I could smell something rotten here and it angered me beyond words. *This is my country you scoundrels are mucking with!*

"Not much. What's new with you?"

Not an original greeting I realize, but it gets the job done.

Paul and I do a lot of trail riding together. He's a classic example of poor off-road riding technique. Doesn't do anything by the book, his posture totally incompatible with the accepted and proven norm. But it all works.

The first snowfall of the season, Paul had something new. I heard a wild racket coming from the vicinity of my driveway and looked out the side window to see him sitting on a filthy Norton Commando, his usual impish grin punctuated by a thin, odorous cigar. There was about 15 cm of snow on the ground.

No way I could ever get Paul into a column, physically or otherwise. The man is big. Picture a cross between Pierre Radisson and John Belushi, with maybe a touch of Santa Claus thrown in for good measure.

Anyway, Paul had his helmet on that day, the yellow pudding-bowl one that's never strapped, a shirt, an official true-north padded vest, jeans, and rubber lace-up work boots, unlaced. The Norton was a new toy.

Its valves rattled and smoke poured out the exhaust along with the lovely standard Norton noises as I tossed snow underneath to mop up the oil leaking out of everywhere. Paul just grinned, his weight straining the under-inflated rear tire. I think he swiped the plate off his XR to ride the Norton around the block to my place.

The big advantage in having only three or four metres through which to view the world is that it allows a mind to focus on things and not get confused by surrounding issues. Sometimes distractions, particularly when dressed up in motherhood garb, tend to cloud reasoning with "facts and logic" at the expense of truth. What is really happening?

When the lake freezes over, most of the snowmobilers and ATV riders whizzing along the ice past my gap wear helmets. I think this is great. In fact, I've been accused on more than one occasion of putting on my helmet simply to look at bikes. And while reality isn't quite that severe, I openly admit to being a pro-helmet fanatic. Yet, when I look at Paul, a rebellious independent soul with a history of motorcycling, from chopped Harleys to two-stroke triples, a man who has always made a good living for his family despite the thick goo of government regulations that discourage free enterprise, and the equally demoralizing anti-efficiency campaigns of big business, I find myself questioning the morality of laws that attempt to force independence into a mould.

Forget writing in to tell me all the inarguable advantages of protective head gear. I already know them. That's why I wear the best helmet I can buy, and preach to all within range to do likewise. The issue here is freedom. We as a people are rapidly giving up our right of self-determination, our right to take risks, and our right to function as individuals, all in exchange for a governmental guaranteed baby-sitting service. Whether the issue be helmets, family allowance cheques, or the inability to get insurance because those leech-like lawyers have driven the rates beyond reach with lawsuits beyond reason, we, you and I, are selling our souls to the devil. And worse still, we are also selling our children's souls in the bargain.

Granted this may be a narrow view of the world, but what do you expect from a three or four metre gap between buildings?

Adding to the confusion, just for fun

January 1987

Around about now, magazine editors all over the world are busy poring over the statistics—luggage capacity, quarter mile times, top speed, fuel economy, price, dry weight, wet weight, roll on, and on and on, sifting through the data in search for the "Bike Of The Year!" or "Best Baker's Dozen!" or whatever. But can that many bikes really be the best? What results is an awards banquet confusion.

That's why I decided to come up with my own annual awards system. The market for confusion is obviously healthy, and confusion is a condition that has long been recognized as a specialty of mine.

Nineteen eighty-six was a banner year for me as far as riding somebody else's bikes was concerned. Thanks to the distributors and

Awards of merit for anything are a bit of a farce. Even when legitimately judged on merit alone, that merit is the highly subjective opinion of the judges, all of whom are brilliant and perceptive experts in the recipient's mind, or a bunch of ignorant clowns obviously bankrolled by some unnamed interested party in the mind of the unjustifiably overlooked. One reason annual awards are popular among magazines is that such awards usually result in more advertising for the award-giving magazines. I don't think that happened in this case.
—Max

the gang at head office, I sampled nearly every motorcycle whose picture I drooled over during the cold of last January, and then some. Everything from the world's fastest, quickest, whateverest street bikes, dirt bikes, customs, touring machines—hey, I had a great time! So what's my pick of the crop?

First, the ground rules.

To eliminate all bias on my part, none of my own bikes is eligible. Also, none of the winners is to be chromed from wheel to wheel and used as an eye-catching cover shot. Examples of each have to be available in the Canadian marketplace. Only machines that I have ridden this past year will be considered. And spec sheets and statistics get chucked into the trash can, because all that sacred cow-dung means zip when you get right down to the essential reason to ride—fun.

So without further ado, I proudly present (in no particular disorder) "The Four Funnest Motorcycles I Rode in 1986."

• The Harley-Davidson Heritage Softail: Riding this bike was a treat, the epitome of vintage Harley experience, only without the creaks and leaks of old machinery. Arms and legs out in the wind, floorboards, an army-surplus brake pedal, a great huge chrome headlight to watch yourself race past the clouds in, the chug-chug-chug omnipotence of a big air-cooled V-twin—even four-lane expressway travel was a blast! No other motorcycle recreates the past as well as this one, and it does so while sacrificing very little to the present. And because it's *soooo* gosh darn pretty, just looking at it was fun.

• The Honda Fat Cat: We'll probably lose some more ads over this one, but anyway, the Fat Cat looks stupid. I'm not even sure if it qualifies as a motorcycle, but this is my annual awards here, so I don't care. I do know that I sure laughed a lot whenever I rode it. And even after testing it, I still puzzle over how anything slower than a new bottle of ketchup could be so darn much fun, but it is. The Fat Cat amazes by going virtually anywhere, no skill required, thank you very much. What Honda has here is a trials machine for the incompetent. What a rider gets here is a heck of a good time. It may look weird, but as long as its putt-putt-putt keeps bringing on the ha-ha-has, who cares?

• The Yamaha SRX600: Early Sunday morning, when the sun is still crimson on the horizon and breath mists up in the air, a favourite road beckons, its hills and curves waiting, silent and empty. You want to ride briskly, not race.

You want to ride a motorcycle, not a corporation's engineering ego. The bike must be light and nimble, and you have to see the engine, and feel it, and hear it, for the engine is a motorcycle's soul. You ride alone. Single. The SRX600 single, because it is perhaps the ultimate early Sunday morning motorcycle. Even the kickstarter seems right, as if buttons would interfere with the message. And the message is pure fun.

• Dave Mascioli's 1967 Honda 65: This year, motorcycle day at the local museum, I asked Dave if I could sit on his restored 65. I started laughing as soon as I took it off the centrestand, continued laughing as Dave operated the kickstarter with a flick of his wrist, paused briefly as everyone nearby stopped talking so we could hear if the engine was running, and then laughed some more as I accelerated—no wait, the word "accelerate" does not really apply here—as I gathered up what appeared to be forward motion to a frantic pace of about 20 km/h. Scary, huh? And a genuine hoot. Thanks, Dave.

There was a bunch of other bikes that impressed for a variety of reasons, some of which I would dearly like to own, and I'm certain they'll end up on somebody else's awards list, but these four are the ones that scored highest on my official Giggle Frequency Indicator. I make no apologies for their lack of spec-sheet techno-status, or any shortcomings in practicality, accepted performance criteria, or even affordability, for each was chosen by a chuckle. If both my wallet and garage were big enough, each would form part of my ideal motorcycle playpen.

Now that sounds like fun to me.

Note: Although the bikes chosen here differ somewhat—not only from each other, but also from most of the other bikes available at the time—the point is that there really aren't any bad bikes.

—Max

Mass transit isn't healthy for people and other living things

February 1987

Before your eyes recognize what it is, your nose

does. That's one of the costs of being a motorcyclist. You not only smell the flowers first, you also smell the manure. Ahead, a tractor-trailer struggles around an uphill corner, its load of cattle in transit mooing madly, frightened and disoriented. Unfortunately, economic necessity dictates that this cargo of future hamburger must be crammed into tight quarters, with no regard shown for comfort or the individual concerns of passengers.

Beginning to experience hot flashes of déjà vu? Could you have been a cow in your previous life? I suppose it's possible, but more likely, the smells, the uncomfortable feelings, and the paranoia you are recognizing belong to the present world. It was, you see, this

Memorable, as Max describes a flight to Brazil where he'd arranged a visit and test ride with the Amazonas factory. The entire episode, including the main feature in the same issue of Cycle Canada, was truly bizarre. It only took place because Max had won the airfare to Brazil in a contest.
—Bruce Reeve, editor of Cycle Canada magazine

I thrive on bizarre.
—Max

no-frills method of transporting livestock that mass transit chose as its model.

Mass transit is the antithesis of motorcycling. It is the loss of freedom, of individuality, of control, and of fun. And like the prototype, most modern examples also stink.

I recently flew to Brazil on a 747. A big airplane has some definite advantages over surface-bound forms of mass transit. For one thing, it is the fastest manner of getting someplace far away, which theoretically cuts down on the exposure time to those cattle-car abuses. It also banks around corners, and the sensation of acceleration, while no match for 120 horsepower unleashed between your legs, is at least interesting. Certainly better than an overloaded bus wallowing around in the passing lane. And those adjustable air nozzles that blast reprocessed cigarette smoke and the like down on to the passengers, when combined with the noise of jet engines, make it possible to fart with complete impunity, a definite advantage over crowded trains and buses. So much for the positive side.

In the past, I have flown and found it quite tolerable. Not so this time. The airline involved, Aerolineas Argentinas, made life bouncing between airports so grim that it wasn't long before some of its captives began referring to it as Aero-anus Intestinitis.

The list of atrocities included consistently boarding long after we were supposed to have taken off; a stop-over in New York (an atrocity in itself) where we were herded into a stark, unclean, windowless room housing rows of vandalized chairs and posters extolling the virtues of Woody Allen's favourite city, and then confined to this hole for two hours without forewarning, explanation or apology; in-flight food that at best could only be described as durable (I never knew rubber-ham could be served so many times in a day); stewardesses who, by some unfortunate misalignment of the stars and planets, all seemed to have been suffering from a severe bout of PMS; overhead lockers that sprung open whenever we hit a bit of turbulence, dumping their contents all over those seated below; free cigarettes handed out to everyone in the no smoking areas; a wild, aborted landing, again with no apologies or explanations to calm our fears of joining cattle compatriots in hamburger land; and the return-flight endurance test at Rio de Janeiro aeroporto.

This particular atrocity began with an hour wait at the seat allocation desk before anything turned up, which wasn't a total loss as we had to hang around the airport for five hours anyway waiting for the next flight out, so we pigged out on yummie Brazilian chocolate while watching the freaks parade by. Boarding was late, as expected, and then we sat in the plane for about half an hour while a great banging and clanging went on down in the bowels of our 747.

Eventually the racket retired and our pilot announced that due to air-traffic congestion, there would be a 15-minute delay before take-off. But instead of departing, the repairs started up again, this time with a much bigger hammer. Our sewer-shaped sanctuary shook and rattled for the next two hours, its sweating occupants taxing the plane's air-recirculation system as a determined ground crew pounded away at the mystery problem. No apologies. No explanations. No smiles from the stewardesses.

Sometime during the wee hours of the next morning, the aircraft managed to free itself from Rio and make way for Miami, which at least has a hospitable airport to sit in while work crews stuffed the plane's pantry with more tributes to extended shelf-life.

Perhaps the most ironic part of this airborne fiasco was that it was booked through a travel agency that boldly goes by the name "Joy of Travel." I wonder if they do any of the travel arrangements for the Ontario Stockyards?

The next time you happen upon a truck load of tomorrow's roast beef, instead of turning up your nose and speeding past, toot the horn and flash a salute. No living creature deserves such abuse.

Mass transit sacrifices too much in the name of efficiency, forgetting one major difference between people and livestock–if all goes well, the humans might come back for another ride.

That's why my garage is full of motorcycles.

On the gas and sideways, sliding to infinity

April 1987

The transitions between Canadian seasons can be a real drag, an unpredictable time of year that sees Mother Nature struggling through her quarterly identity crisis, no help from the weatherman thank you very much. It's neither one thing nor the other, not black or white, winter or spring, war or peace–just a crazy climatic schizophrenia. For instance, today, five days after the official advent of spring, CBC of the Near North is calling for rain, snow, freezing rain, clouds, and sunshine.

All bases covered. But in what? And do we really want to know?

Fortunately, life at these times isn't always a total loss. Once in a while, this capricious nature of Nature can produce a genuine treat, like a late Indian Summer or, as it did this past weekend, two days

Motorcycling can reveal some beautiful places that might otherwise go unnoticed. This is one of those places.
—Max

of heavy rain followed by an evening of bring-in-the-brass-monkey temperatures, followed in turn by a day of sunshine.

Now some of you are probably wondering how anyone other than an African drought victim with a hate-on for warm weather could find happiness in that weather recipe, but keep in mind that at this time of year, up our way, such an event turns the lake to near glass.

It's a condition that never lasts long, and serves principally as a prelude to spring break-up, so those who are interested have to move fast. The lake will soon be unusable until around mid-May.

Monday night and small groups of skaters trace along the shoreline from the Government Dock to who knows where. Peter, our town's token marine biologist, drills a hole through a metre of ice to take samples of lake water a hundred metres out from his home. And we, the ice bikers, embark on a moonlight ride to the islands.

We knew it would be fun, but we never anticipated the magic.

Out on the lake, studded tires lay down tracks that sparkle like diamond threads spinning off a half-dozen free-rolling spools. Our lines criss-cross and weave, forming a giant two-dimensional ice macram as we sweep through an endless series of throttle-controlled slides, first right, then left, one after another after another. Under the cloud-swept moon and stars, we perform this crude and exhilarating ballet for no audience but ourselves. It's a grand night for a moondance, my friend.

We ride fast, yet, with no reference points save the moonlight reflecting across the ice, the sensation of speed is lost. There is just the wind and those long, endless slides.

Just this side of the islands, a huge pressure crack slices across the lake, preventing us from reaching our destination. It doesn't matter. Destination is no longer our goal, we're after the ultimate slide, an extended trip through open space, like a free-falling sky-diver who never has to worry about opening the chute.

In a separate world off in the distance, the shoreline city lights flicker like a birthday cake for an old friend. Make a wish and *sliiiide*.

It's pure magic. Not some stage-show hocus-pocus, but the real thing. A subtle glow rises from the ice, like black silver, coating us in its spell. We know we can ride forever without hitting a thing. Not even a snow bank. Try to imagine five hundred metres, sideways, flat out in third gear, going and going and going, yet never gone.

It is glorious. In the magic of moonlight, we have broken the forever barrier.

It is also eerie, almost chilling, not from the cold, but from the sense of total strangeness. Nothing I have ever tasted before has prepared me for this. Growling black dots slice through a night without borders, edges, or obstructions. During one incredible slide I thought would never end, an out-of-control spirit burst from within, screaming *yahooo*! into my helmet. In the overall cosmic scheme of things, it was but a mere speck of time, a brief moment of intense excitement witnessed only by myself, the moon, and Mother Nature. But jeez, what a high.

I make no claims to being "at one with nature" during all this madness, or any other such philosophical crap. Who wants to be at one with a schizophrenic anyway? Besides, our mode of transport is far too raucous for such lofty aspirations or aspirations. But. There is still a peculiar sort of fusion, as the tools of man are put to play in the theatre which nature has provided, a setting which at best won't be repeated for at least another year. No, this is not philosophy at work here, simply magic.

The morning after, as I write this, the snow is turning to rain and the lake is suffering a severe meltdown. The season is officially over. But hey, what a finale! These are memories that will sit forever tucked into the corners of a smile.

Transitions. There's a month of climatic depression ahead as we wait for spring to blossom into biking weather. The only thing fit to ride now is the bus. But who knows? Maybe Mother Nature will toss out yet another surprise for us, like a week of warm sunshine. Or perhaps a hurricane.

You never know what to expect from a schizoid.

Boneheads, meatheads and pig-headed bicycloids

May 1987

Some time ago, an organization called the Citizens for Safe Cycling called the office to ask for permission to reprint one of my columns in its newsletter. Chris Knowles took the call, phoned me, and in a moment of weakness no doubt brought on by all this attention (blush), I consented. It was a decision I found myself regretting almost immediately.

Why? On the surface, it seems that only an engine separates our vehicular interests, but the differences go far beyond any chosen means of propulsion. While motorcyclists have often been scorned by the common man's media for their apparent anti-social behaviour and indifference to safety, in reality only the Hell's Angels have got much of an edge in this regard

I didn't sit down to write this rant, it just sort of spilled out of my computer. I was merely an amused bystander. Happens sometimes.

The column stirred up no shortage of amusing controversy, just one of the many pleasures I derive from writing Around the Bend.

—Max

over the average holier-than-thou granola-brained bicyclist.

City bicyclists tend to be the most discourteous, pig-headed bunch of boneheads on the road, demanding all the privileges of both pedestrians and motorists while showing no consideration for the rules and responsibilities that come as part and parcel of street usage. They consistently and willfully ignore every law of the road as they scrape the paint off innocent vehicles while bouncing through congested traffic; then these pedalling potty-heads have the audacity to scream at anyone who, in the course of operating their own vehicle sanely and legally, might obstruct their sacrosanct path.

Only fractionally less obnoxious than these dolts are the "racers." This muscle-bound band of morons insists on cluttering rural highways by riding four abreast, five deep, at about half the recognized speed limit. And usually, some dutiful wifey follows close behind in the "I-don't-like-cars" family rust bucket, four-way flashers just a humming, with the standard WARNING! BABY ON BOARD sticker plastered over the rear window defogger. Racing be damned, this intrusion constitutes a road-block!

These arrogant meatheads haunt some of the best backroads that surround metropolitan areas. And pray you never have the misfortune to encounter one of their start/finish lines! Here, the pack parks beat-up Pintos, Ladas and Fiats along both sides of an already narrow road before strutting about in their stretch elastic black underwear, refusing to move for any traffic that doesn't have a bicycle rack strapped to its roof rack or bumper.

The bicycling movement (similar in concept to a bowel movement) is saturated with contempt for anyone engaged in any other form of travel. There exists a thoroughly unjustified air of superiority that these space invaders try to cultivate based upon the premise that this is indeed a wonderful thing that they are doing for mankind.

"I'm not using any of the world's non-renewable natural resources in my $800 imported mountain bicycle built in some oppressive shop using the modern equivalent of slave labour, and look how healthy I am too!"

In actual fact, what they are really cultivating is confrontation, something they share in common with all groups who claim to have some deity, motherhood, and righteousness on their side. And as an aside, that air about them is actually body odour.

Lord knows, any motorcyclist who conducted himself in the incredibly anti-social manner that bicyclists get away with would have his license suspended for life, and likely that of his children and grandchildren too, plus face incarceration for at least eternity. Maybe even longer.

But what about the bicycle touring crowd? Not a bad bunch on the average. Normally, they ride single file, as if they realize that the road is a shared public transit system, and that they are but a very small segment of its users. These folks, I give a wide berth to when I pass. They respect my rights; I respect theirs.

Why the difference in attitude between those that confront and those that are willing to share? It's in the choice of seats. It seems that the hard, thin butt-basher that the racers and city terrorists prefer is having a pronounced effect on the only operative cerebral part of their bodies, damaging what little intellect they could have once laid claim to.

That's why I joined the Citizens for Systematic Cyclicide, a group dedicated to the elimination of these mindless bicycloids through such tactics as unsignalled lane changes, the opportune opening of a car door, the unsuspected blast of a horn, buzzing, sticking out your tongue, whatever it takes to free our roads of the bicycling blight. Let us force the bicycloids to revert to beating their cats for entertainment, or maybe thumbing through their back issues of *Mother Earth News*. Only then will we, and our children, be free to travel without harassment, intimidation, or obstruction, whether walking, driving, riding a motorcycle, or even out on our bicycles.

I never did discover what column it was the Citizens For Safe Cycling wanted. They didn't have the courtesy to send me a copy of their newsletter, which I guess should have been expected. Doubt if we'll get any requests on this one.

Tales from the Agent Orange Death Wagon

June 1987

Even though it's obviously got too many wheels, the pickup still holds a strong spiritual link to motorcycling. For one thing, it can carry bikes in the back. But there's more to the link than this plebian transportation of the goodies. A pickup, like a bike, can own a good dose of genuine character.

We used to have a one-ton four-wheel-drive GMC, an industrial cast-off painted construction-company orange, with a cab crammed to the dashboard with fishing rods, welding helmets, motorcycle helmets, boots, jackets, gloves, goggles, the tackle box, etc., plus one of the North's finest collections of almost empty Tim Horton's coffee cups. It usually took me fifteen minutes to dig out the seat belt, and ten to find the stick shift.

I have had the pleasure of experiencing the close friendship of some wonderfully rebellious characters, all of whom in some way have helped to shape my warped outlook on life. Pal Paul is a good example, this being another tale of our mutual exploits, with more connecting of the disorganized dots of the universe.
—Max

Legally, the truck belonged to my friend Paul. He used it to travel back and forth to work, parked it in his driveway, and paid the insurance. But that was irrelevant. Its main purpose in life was to cart battle-weary enduros up the north highway in pursuit of our weekend mud bath.

Admittedly, this high-mileage special was a bit of a slug, its horses suffocating under a diet of propane (Paul's idea, not mine), but power wasn't the only luxury it lacked. A heater, suspension, tires with tread—stuff like that would have been nice too. And then there was this thing about the brakes.

Once, while hauling home the usual aftermath of a Sunday-morning ride up the Hydro line, we charged down Thibault Hill in heavy debate as to who pushed who out of which mud hole, when it came to our attention that the brakes weren't really braking.

To put this into perspective, Thibault is one of those long escarpment cuts over which hangs a permanent odour of overheated brake linings. At the bottom lies my home town—Bargain Harold's, the wife, kid, friends, and all that. And a major intersection of the Trans-Canada Highway. Had our truck been equipped with a CB, we would have had the makings of a classic country and western tragedy.

Instead, as we rushed toward approaching doom discussing what new bikes we were going to get (surely those beat-up wonders out back would be destroyed in the crash), I was sufficiently moved to christen this troublesome truck.

Space here is restricted, so let me just say that all survived the adventure (what an amazing escape!), including the truck's new name—the Agent Orange Death Wagon.

Agent Orange was like a faithful dog. A crippled one with asthma. Go anywhere for you just because it didn't know any better.

Unfortunately, the day Paul needed a mobile welding rig, Agent Orange was sitting next to his shop, so off came the pickup bed and on went the engines and cords and clamps and oxy-acetylene bottles (why are these things called bottles?)... no more room for the bikes.

So we began using my car and trailer. Nice family sedan, empty ash trays, comfort and warmth—it just wasn't the same anymore.

In Agent Orange, conversation was dominated by what new surprises the beast might have in store for us this week, interspersed with Paul's defence of what a great truck it really was. Sure, it could have used a live-in maid, but that crowded mess was a great nesting ground for the absurd, like the time we figured that if we could just find a way to make the world temporarily spin a little faster, we might build up sufficient momentum to clear the next hill.

In the car, we briefly made comment on how well the heater and defroster worked, and the ease with which the windows rolled up and down, then slid into other mundane topics, like how the whole world is going to hell in a hand cart. The undeniable comfort we basked in seemed to provide a better atmosphere for bitching than brilliant theories.

So Paul bought another pickup. In contrast to Agent Orange, this one is luxury—brakes, a wonderful and glutonous 7.5 litre V8 that probably gives one unemployed Albertan his job back every time it fires up, power assisted this and that, running boards, plastic woodgrain inserts, a growing collection of almost-empty Tim Horton's coffee cups, and a couple of PROUD TO BE A NEWFIE stickers attesting to some previous owner's East Coast heritage. About the only thing missing is a name.

Assigning names to inanimate objects is a tricky business. Some folks label each car they buy, and each motorcycle, boat, shoe, carpet, and so forth as soon as they can provide proof of ownership. For me, something devoid of life has to possess a lot of character and familiarity before being blessed with anything so personal as a name. Brian Mulroney, for instance, should never have been named. And maybe a few of the new bikes too. Anyway, come some appropriate moment, when inspiration collides with circumstance, Paul's new truck will inevitably get a name.

It's only a matter of time, because getting there is part of the fun again. Not as much of a hoot as bouncing through the bush on the bikes mind you, but it still makes for a good warm-up.

Note: Brian Mulroney was the prime minister of Canada at the time I wrote this column. He remains one of the very few people I actually despise, and will remain so until one of us kicks the bucket. Over to you, Bri...
—Max

A nutcase on the road to Showcase delirium

March 1988

At the back of this magazine each and every month is a tribute to insanity called Showcase. You can't miss it, a colour photo featuring some bizarre motorcycle mutation of questionable origin. Below the motorized creature lies a brief description of how the owner took a perfectly good motorcycle and turned it into a temperamental bride of Frankenstein with a face only its creator could love, worth about a third of the heaps of hard-earned paycheques invested. Obviously there has got to be a nut loose here somewhere and I don't think it's on the bike. Maybe they should re-title the page Nutcase.

Showcase is a monthly record of the disease known as "project bike." Some innocent buys a motorcycle designed by engineers with years

I recently sold the bike described in this column—where is, as is—an unrealized dream of ideas and mechanical bits that failed to assemble, progress ending shortly after I began building my own home, the dream ending somewhat later when deteriorating health met reality and declared this dream dead. Fortunately, there's no shortage of other dreams to take up the slack.
—Max

of training and experience and all the advantages of computer aids (another disease), then promptly decides he can make major improvements by working on it with a few hand tools. In his spare time. In the basement. Fourteen coats of powdered epoxy paint for the bike and a straight jacket for the owner, please.

Years ago, I bought a brand-new 1978 Yamaha XS650E. The XS650 is a sometimes cantankerous, semi-anemic, vertical twin that vibrates better than a sex-shop toy and handles like a drunken Carlsberg Clydesdale. But mine sure looked like a proper motorcycle, with wire wheels and a kickstart. I liked it a lot. Truth was, all it needed was a bit of fine tuning—a couple of braces here and there, a little more power, shocks... see the pattern?

In a rare, fleeting moment of sanity, I sold the XS before reaching the point of no return, replacing it with the latest ultracycle of the year, thereby saving myself a lot of money and aggravation while gaining a quantum leap in performance. Yet the thrill of this new whoopee bike was not lasting, so I sold it too, bought a wreck and rebuilt it. That's something I will never do again until the next time because for all the hours and money squandered, I could have built a real nifty project bike.

Shortly after this frightening realization, I saw an ad in the *Northern Daily Misprint* for a basket-case XS650, a '78 just like my old one. "*Sold!*" cried insanity. Awash in foolish sentimentality, I paid too much for nostalgia and carted the rusted hulk home in the trunk of my car.

I think the madness is worst during those hazy moments lying in bed when the mind slips into a semi-conscious state of wakefulness. It was there that I first saw my beautiful vertical air-cooled twin with traditional wires and a kickstart, rearsets, clubman solo seat, aluminum swingarm off some derelict dirt bike, a fat fork salvaged from a modern sportbike or Gold Wing... whoa, what's this kid on?

I called up Rick Andrews, fellow member of the *Cycle Canada* Contibuting Editor's Guild, to get some expert advice on reality. Rick works on a lot of the new superbike stuff, so I was prepared for a few snickers. In other words, I was ill-prepared, because he thought fixing up an XS650 was a great idea. In fact, somewhere he might even have some 750 sleeves for it, and did I want some old wire wheels off a TZ750? Fixing the handling was easy, you just get an aluminum swingarm off an old dirt bike and a new front end from a modern sportbike or Gold Wing...

Hey wait a minute, has somebody been tapping my late-night hallucinations?

Being an impoverished writer, my wallet couldn't stand the cost of brand-spanking new, so I popped into Ontario Cycle Salavage and T.O. Cycle Salvage, the east-west of Toronto battered-bike bits. Sheepishly, I revealed my modest plans to responses of blah, blah, blah, all excited, nobody's building specials anymore, talked for an hour before we even discussed what stuff I needed.

This was getting ridiculous. Even my friends failed me, staring at the collection of corrosion spread beneath the basement wash lines while telling me straight-faced how neat it all was. Give me a break guys, it's just the skeleton of a dumb old motorcycle run aground among its own diseased innards! Jeez.

So I bought another one for spares, a '71. When I got it home, I realized that it was too good to merely strip for parts, so Stuart Livesacrossfromtheinlaws adopted it, mumbling something about vintage road racing (a similar disorder to "project bike," but with the bonus of broken bones thrown in). I've got a lead on some rumours of a couple of other basketcases going begging somewhere, supposedly, and Willie-down-the-road has a pair of neato Mikunis from the remains of a highly modified triple (the third carb was destroyed in the fire), and Kal Saari tells me that his fibreglass replica Norvil racing tank for Nortons will probably fit, and... oh dear.

This is bad. I've even got the colours picked out, but won't tell anybody in case they steal my brilliant idea. Project paranoia.

Around here, they call it Showcase, but it should be re-titled.

Throwing our helmets into the political fray

June 1988

Having just returned from Ottawa, I can say

with some authority that it is true—Parliament Hill is abuzz with rumours of an upcoming election. This doesn't leave a lot of time.

The idea of a single-issue political party is not new. Since confederation, both the Liberals and Conservatives seemed to have done quite well by simply headlining greed (the Managing Editor here won't let me talk about what is keeping the NDP in the headlines). So the political ground has been broken. Canada is ready for the Pro-Bike Party, and here's what I'm going to do when elected (didn't I mention that part?).

First the non-controversial items: All lawyers, judges, and mainstream politicians will be gathered up and bussed to the Humane

My continued editorial efforts to prod governments into working for a better world notwithstanding, politics remains all about power, greed, and self-interest. So why not get involved? I asked.
—Max

Society where they will be put down. I know there might be one or two acceptable humans in that bunch, but we haven't got the time to go searching for a few good apples in a bucket of compost, so it's roses for every one of them.

Any insurance company found to be charging fees in excess of the actual risks for motorcycle coverage will have its executives burned at the stake (stock up on your marshmallows). Not wanting to break with all political traditions of the past, the resultant job openings will be filled with friends of the government (FOG).

All vehicle operators found drunk at the helm will be shot on the spot. As a gesture of heartfelt sympathy, a complimentary balloon-a-gram will be sent to the pickled stiff's family to notify survivors as to where the body and vehicle can be picked up before storage charges get out of hand.

And now to the serious bike stuff. With asinine lawsuits assigned to history, the responsibility of risk will naturally fall upon whoever chooses to take the risk (what a concept!). Everything has a price, including freedom. Pro-Bike will leave it up to individuals as to whether they want to pay it or not. So helmets will be mandatory only for news media journalists, who have to wear them backwards at all times because they never see very far anyway. For those fearing a sudden road rash of Ride Free lobotomies, please remember that this could give us a whole new sector from which to choose qualified civil servants.

While on the topic, those sensationalist no-mind junk-journalists who insist on smearing motorcycles and ATVs across the front pages for the ignorant public whenever a new menace is needed to boost ratings or readership will be sentenced to 10 years as transport-driver training-program pylons, all the while repeating, "Just the facts please, m'am."

On the other side of the reality coin, motorcyclists who continually fret over the "image of motorcycling" will be given free counselling.

It will be illegal for anyone to purchase a motorcycle whose hp exceeds his or her IQ.

It will be illegal to use the word "domestic" in conjunction with Harley-Davidsons at any motorcycle event in Canada.

Under the Visually Offensive Motorcycle Act, it will be illegal to re-sell an ugly motorcycle. Those who bought them will have to keep them. It's a fitting punishment for falling prey to some inspirational blob that any notion of good taste would have deleted from the company CAD-CAM before it ever got into injection-moulded plastic and porous Arrowroot metal castings, let alone somebody's neighbourhood.

Police-department ticket quotas for traffic violations will be banned, to be replaced with charge quotas for real crimes. The role of the police will then change from that of the villain in pursuit of citizens to that of the good guy in pursuit of criminals.

Expect some serious changes in the day-to-day workings of government too. Once sworn in as your PM, I will immediately switch that title to AM because I don't like to stay up late. Also, you can count on drastic cutbacks in government spending. For example, instead of traipsing off hither and thither on expensive jumbo-jet forays to exotic destinations, whenever possible, the Pro-Bike Party will ride. And the only money spent on government advertising will be for "wish you were here" postcards mailed to local constituents back home. The resultant dollars saved from this frugality will be used to subsidize bike prices.

Once back from our first World Tour for International Cooperation in Twisty Roads and Abolition of Speed Limits, government limos will be swapped for sidecars, the Senate will be replaced by the Downchild Blues Band, and a motocross track will be set up around Parliament Hill for the revamped version of the famed changing of the guards. Rumours won't be the only thing abuzz on the Hill when Pro-Bike takes over.

And how's this for an election slogan: There's Always Varoom For Improvement? Like it? Oh well. Maybe we'll come up with something better before the election is called. Send in your suggestions. And be sure to get out and support your local riding. Every town should have a Pro-Bike Party.

Gamesmanship and the traffic stream

August 1988

I had just ridden 350 km non-stop. No stop for gas, no stop for a pee, not even a pause to rest my weary paws. All the way from Northern Ontario to the Don Valley Parkway in Toronto. Then I stopped.

Stuck in the constipated lanes of this supposed expressway, with no tape-deck to listen to except the guy's seven or eight cars ahead of me, my helmet began to fill with profundities. That's the trouble with full-face helmets—there's no place for the thoughts to filter out.

Have you ever tried to look at a big city objectively? Ignore the colour of the air and the garbage strewn about for the moment; what do you see? Traffic. Doesn't matter where you look, it's everywhere and constant, and it is fascinating how city dwellers cope with it.

You can't always avoid life's dreck but you can at least find ways to deal with it. Perhaps it's no surprise that for me a motorcycle is usually involved in dealing with the dreck.

—Max

The name of the game is vehicular hopscotch. Notice that the lane you are in is always the slowest one. If you can somehow manage to squeeze into the line of whizzing autos next to you, that lane then slows down and the one you just left speeds up. It's just like playing the stock market. And every once in a while there is a Black Monday—the big crash. That's when you wish you'd invested in a train ticket.

Nobody in a big city sleeps. Those driving around don't sleep (usually), and the others can't because of the noise from all the traffic, so they get up and go for a drive. To relax. The big plus to this endless circle of inner-city internal-combustion commotion is that you can let loose with the after-effects of a home-baked bean dinner anywhere, anytime, and no one will ever hear you. And the pollution hides the odour. But back to the hopscotch.

Nobody ever wins vehicular hopscotch. The object is not to get anywhere; that's simply one of the game's interesting side effects. The object is to irritate. Traffic pros can pump up the community blood pressure high enough to cause a nose bleed and fry a pacemaker. Now, I have no trouble with that admirable goal; gosh knows it's one I have adhered to in this column for years. But lately, perhaps in the last two years, there has been a new twist added to the game. It is now quite legit, preferable even, to include oneself in this creative process of aggravation.

It is a most peculiar phenomenon. People fume and steam, putting themselves in situations that can only lead to self-inflicted frustration. Grown yuppies in Jags and BMWs, commoners in delivery vans, housepersons toting the kids home from daycare, they all take time out of their busy day to roll down the window and toss out a few choice insults and rude gestures at each other because neither antagonist nor victim can drive worth a damn. Sometimes, they even exchange business cards with their terse remarks jotted down on the back. This allows them to get in touch later, at a mutually convenient time, to continue this barter of abuse, or perhaps use the cellular phone so as not to overwork the car's climate-control system by letting outside air in. Push, shove, bumper, fender, squeeze, heart-attack city, save a second, lose a minute, go home and beat the family. It's a good life all in all.

So why not try mass transit? I did. Once. The first thing I noticed on the subway was that nearly everyone was standing, though there were plenty of empty seats. Weird? Not for an old dirt rider like myself.

I quickly surmised that those sitting were mass transit novices, while those standing were obviously the pros. You always stand when approaching a rough section. So I stood and waited for the bumpy bits with the rest of my fellow riders. No bumps were forthcoming. Sensing I was the brunt of a clever and well-planned conspiracy to make a fool of the new guy in town, I stomped off the subway with an "Oh yeah?" kind of response and returned to traversing the city on a motorcycle.

Ah, much better. The ticket to a quick, or at least not painfully slow, blast through Clogcity is my pal, the sadly neglected dual-purpose motorcycle. It sits high, letting you peer over the top of traffic bickering. You can sneak through teensy-weensy gaps, you can accelerate and veer out of harm's way and the way of mindless drivers, and you can effortlessly ride over manhole covers, potholes, beer cans, bicyclists—in fact, most of the crud that is apt to impinge upon one's journey through the streets of life. And you don't even have to roll a window down to offer helpful driving tips to the boneheads who cut you off.

Ideally, the urban dual-purpose should be about 250 cc, light to flick around, and physically small so you don't have to breathe in when things get a little close. You still won't be able to ride non-stop anywhere in the city, especially when using the comprehensive expressway system, but it does get you where you want to go quicker, and with less aggravation. But is this still playing the game? Do you care?

Spruce trees and speed limits owe it all to saps

September/October 1988

I was out trail riding the other day on my dual-purpose donk when I was attacked by aliens posing as spruce trees. This was not the first time I had fallen victim to such encounters, and upon reflection under ice packs, a pattern emerged.

In each instance, I was tired. My mind was not on the task at hand the way it should have been. And, on each occasion where my body sustained damage, I was going slow, taking it easy. Deductive reasoning then leads us to conclude that one should have a nap when tired, and always ride fast.

It all has to do with awareness. Obviously, a person is apt to be more aware of his surroundings when awake, but what has speed got to do with it? The mind tends to become complacent when not

Another popular theme among Around the Bend writers, or themes among the Around the Bend writer. Whatever. Humanity sure does get stuck in its ways in the pursuit of mediocrity, eh?
—Max

challenged. It takes a deliberate and continual effort to prevent the mind from lapsing into a cerebral fog when external inputs are repetitive and of no apparent immediate concern. It's called boredom. Boredom may be the greatest undeclared danger of the 20th century. Riding fast relieves boredom.

Now, I'm not suggesting that everyone start blitzing downtown Main St. full throttle in the name of safety. There is more than enough happening in city traffic to keep a mind occupied at 50 km/h or so. But down a lonesome highway or deserted trail, particularly if any distances are involved, it can become dangerous to maintain artificial and irrelevant limits over long periods of time.

Why 80, 90 or 100 km/h? These limits were established years ago when vehicles couldn't stop or handle. Not only are vehicle performance standards vastly superior now, so are the roads, which only compounds the problem of boredom.

Unfortunately, speed limits have acquired sacred-cow status, to be defended at any cost. Exceed them and you will surely die, or at least be subject to harassment, fines, and increased insurance premiums. Yet *never* has there been any conclusive evidence that speed is the prime cause of accidents. It is all hearsay, which in any other situation would be thrown out of court.

If we accept the holy premise that those who speed are the most dangerous of road users, then it only follows that the most dangerous people on the road would be the police, for they are without doubt the most consistent abusers of the limit in pursuit of its upkeep. That speed is the cause of accidents is an idea born and bred out of ignorance, and maintained by intellectual stagnation. The expense in time and equipment to enforce this senseless law is ridiculous. The fact that it concentrates constabulary efforts on such an imbecilic concept instead of on more productive matters is criminal. But like soldiers in time of war, the constables are "only following orders."

Regrettably, there is some truth to the suggestion that the majority of current road users are not up to the task of higher speed limits. Yet many of them wouldn't be up to it even if limits were universally reduced to 20 km/h! The true cause of accidents is not a factor of speed, but of ability.

Currently, the operation of a motor vehicle is not a question of skill, it is a "right." Licensing standards seem to have been established on the "lowest common denominator" principle, where nearly every person capable of putting his or her X on a voter ballot can also try aiming a vehicle down public roads. Does it make sense that the ability to parallel-park a car or lift a fallen motorcycle should take precedence over accident-avoidance skills?

The quest for excellence does not come from the adoption of mediocre goals. Licensing needs to be totally re-thought, by people capable of thinking. Our obsession of enforcing irrelevant speed limits instead of operator skills is a distraction to safety that contributes more to the problem of accidents than it aids. "Speed kills" and other motherhood phrases like "Strict is Fair" are just a bunch of bilgewater spewed out for the Organization of People Without Functioning Brains. For anyone truly interested in saving lives and not simply the status quo, I submit "Kill Speed Limits" as an alternative.

Realistically, the abolition of highway speed-limits cannot take place until provincial governments decide that road users should show reasonable skill in the operation of a vehicle, a highly unlikely event because of the vast number of voters who would then be deprived of their "right" to maim and destroy, and until federal bureaucrats realize they can follow an independent course to their U.S. counterparts, an equally unlikely circumstance. (Weren't our speed limits lowered immediately after the U.S. did so? Did we not ban three-wheelers immediately after the U.S. did, even though Transport Canada had already tested them and failed to find any flaws?)

Obviously, the influence of aliens in Canada is profound. They may not all pose as spruce trees, but they are *all* equally unwilling to bend in the face of pressing reality–riding fast can prevent accidents. This is not to endorse an abandonment of restraint, but perhaps it is time to start passing the responsibility of it back to the people.

Note: In 2003, Italy chose to raise speed limits, no doubt inspired by the words in this column. Naturally, I take full credit for this rare display of intelligence among politicians.
–Max

A collector of rare and unusual taste

January 1989

It's not like me to be critical, but it's about those guys a few pages back on the masthead. When something dynamic happens around here, they have a moral obligation to pass the news on to you folks, particularly when it concerns a staff member. Well, they've screwed up again.

Back in August of '88, we acquired a new sales rep. Now normally, this wouldn't interest anyone but the rep's mother, but in this case, Jim Aikins (pronounced Jamaicans) is a certified motorcycle collector.

Let me begin at the *Cycle Canada* library, a towering, bulging rack of bike books and yellowing mags that magically arrive here from a variety of journalistically backward locales, like Australia, Britain, U.S.A. and Japan. Even Victoria, B.C., for Pete's sake. This mountain

The world is full of talented people who linger on the edge of discovery. That's life, or fate, or something. Here, I introduced one of the undiscovered who can also be quite funny and insightful.
—Max

of motorcycling mildew threatens to collapse upon my meagre allotment of Toronto real estate, which wouldn't be so bad as long as it took this Trash-80 computer down with it, but anyway, being next to the library, I get to meet all who visit the printed clutter. For example, Jim Aikins.

JA (as he's known on inter-office memos) is a man with a serious mission. Daily, he stalks the library in search of material on the elusive Mondial of Italy. It's not just any Mondial he's after; it's the 50 cc two-stroke bicycle-tired gem of which a row-boat load of approximately six were brought into Canada during the mid-'60s by someone with a bad sense of timing. Or humour. JA has found pictures of the racing model (heady stuff), and a 90 cc four-stroke model, plus a couple of other mutants, but none like the one he so proudly boasts of owning.

With a little prodding, he will also fill you in on the rest of his collection. There's a '70s 250 CZ motocrosser, a '60s Honda C90, a CB350 for parts, and a CL350. Actually, the CL is no longer his. Originally, he bought it for $30 after it had been dragged and flip-flopped behind a pickup truck in an unsuccessful attempt to start it. Details of how the rider fared, if indeed there was one, are not available, but JA has since passed ownership over to his brother in exchange for the $200 JA owed him. JA rationalizes the deal by stating, "He wanted a project; one he couldn't make any mistakes on." Seems to me he already made his first one.

So apparently, the madness runs in the family, which is just as well because not much else seems to. None of the above actually works, which of course is what makes JA a bona fide collector. The other common denominator to the Aikins collection is that most of it is priceless, meaning he didn't pay anything for it. The Mondial he picked up for nothing at an Isetta bubblecar meeting (don't ask what he was doing there) when no one else wanted it, the C90 and CZ were free...

JA has just burst into the editorial department, interrupting the usual intense concentration intrinsic to the production of bullshit, to read a passage from the tattered pages of some *Cycle World* back issue, capturing all the excitement and glory of the 1981 World Mondial Rally. It was attended by a crowd of 31 Mondialites.

Bruce and I recently visited the dungeon in which the Aikins collection is stored. In keeping with the importance of this occasion, JA wore his pseudo-Belstaff slimeskins which he received in a trade for a pile of lumber. The Mondial has not had an easy life. Judging by its appearance, the previous owner used it as a dip stick at a toxic-waste disposal site. But enough of the Mondieu, let me come to the jewel of the collection, the only bike that works.

It's a '73 Honda CB350. JA rides it all year round. Through ice and snow, rain and hail. The seat's torn, the spokes are rusted, the paint on the tank is faded, and it has a big chrome rack projecting out the back. No prima donna parade bike, this one, it's a real motorcycle. And I rode on the back.

JA and I were going to Yamaha's new-model launch and free lunch, so he picked me up at the official *Cycle Canada* rendezvous: the beer store, corner of Lakeshore and Bathurst. "If you feel any wobbling," he warned, "it's not me, it's the bike. The bearings and things are a bit loose." I wonder if the bus will be along soon.

We cruised along Lakeshore, over the Gardiner Expressway, and down the entrance ramp. Leaping passengers, that's the expressway down there Jim! I clung to the rack as the Honda sashayed into the frantic flow of Toronto traffic. There was a sensation, almost like acceleration, but I couldn't quite place it. Hey, look at that, we passed a Corvette! Wonder why he'd want to park there?

We also passed our exit, but no matter, we still arrived early along with the cold cuts. JA parked smack dab right in front of the glittering new Yamahas, dismounted, then stood back proudly as the boys from Yamaha gathered around, speechless. They circled in awe. Then they asked him to move it.

Welcome to *Cycle Canada*, Jim.

Note: As of today (which may not be your today), Jim is the editor of "Motorsport Dealer and Trade," a trade publication produced by Cycle Canada's publisher, Turbopress.
—Max

Excerpts from the notes of a dazed traveller: Part I

May 1989

Like relatives, unexpected snow storms always drop in when you've got to get to someplace quick and you're already late. North of Cambridge, Ontario, by some 450 km, the traffic is clawing for traction at 40 km/h. Anyways, front-ways, side-ways, mine's the sandwich without the mayonnaise, we make Gary Wolf's just after lunch in plenty of time to be attacked by his dog.

Tuesday night at the in-laws, Wednesday back at Central Command trying to read the notes of yesterday's interview, and the weather out in Alberta is so cold it's giving thermometers frostbite. I have yet to pack for the trip to George Lake 400 km northwest of Edmonton. What does one wear to a 24-hour ice race when it's 40 below? Maybe I should call up the

This, and the following column, expose the hectic and often confused side of motorcycle journalism. (It was hell, recalls former ace-reporter.) As with much of my writing, I blame my computer for most of these words. I remain simply the faithful and marginally competent typist at the keyboard.

—Max

other guys and see what they're wearing. Plenty, likely.

Thursday, writing non-stop from 7 a.m. until too late at night, I pause for a few hours sleep before scrambling for the eggs and airport the next morning.

Thousands of feet up in the preferred Boeing of recent crashes, a snotty stewardess who deeply resents being forced to work with humanity served something called "lunch," a gourmet delight of terminally ill vegetables lying limp around what might pass for meat at a senior citizen's cafeteria.

Seen from the air, Alberta is flat, snow-covered, and neatly divided into sections. It looks like a pan of frosted date squares. As we descend, roads become clear—gadzooks, there's a car! They'll never believe this back at the office. I didn't think that anybody out in Alberta knew how to drive.

Seen from the ground, Alberta is flat, snow-covered, and neatly divided into sections. The Edmonton landing-strip is quaint, with flocks of flashing orange lights scurrying about in pretense of serious airport-like business. Between flights, Air Canada's finest unload the very plane in which I survived an in-flight meal and movie. The ground crew are all wrapped up in ear muffs, neck tubes, toques, parkas, mitts, ski pants, mukluks— only their eyes show through the layers. I watch from behind glass, wearing sneakers, jeans and a sweatshirt. Could I be a little underdressed for this environment?

The footwear of choice here is cowboy boots. I think everyone shares the same barber too. As the PA belches out yet another disco arrangement of the classics, I stroll over to the other side of the building to check out the view. Amazingly, it's flat there too. You can actually see the horizon unobscured by high-rise pollution.

There is no announcement of my connecting flight. Well, that's not entirely true. When I and the other four passengers walk out on to the runway and board the Dash 8, a stewardess in Arctic survival gear asks "Okay, is that everybody?"

From the "international" airport, we fly around the city a few times to make the place look big from the air (boy, the things they have to do to impress tourists since Gretzky left), then land at the "municipal" airport in search of more volunteers willing to occupy northbound seats. This is an airline that doesn't put much stock in schedules, but who can blame them when the eagle adorning the Pratt and Whitney engine outside my window is frozen?

We bounce into Grand Prairie where I meet somebody named

Bruce who takes me even farther north in an Aerostar van, pointing out the mystery hill (about the size of the one in my backyard) as we slide all over the icy road to Fairview where I am introduced to a beard and earring whose last name is Bruce, then to somebody else whose first name is Bruce who takes me to his house where I am attacked by his dog. During the next three days, I get frostbite and about 10 hours sleep.

With all that fun dispensed with, I fly Air BC, Air Canada and air sickness back to Toronto, arriving late Tuesday night, then visit the office on Wednesday long enough to empty the in-basket into the waste-basket before I and the mangling editor named Bruce leave for California to test bikes in places where it has just snowed for the first time in recorded history.

American Airlines rewards us with a three-hour detention in depressing, grey Chicago airport because some flight left Dusseldorf one hour late. Finally, they scrape up a stand-in, which we board, but the plane can't take off because its water lines are frozen. Hasn't anybody flown these things in the cold before? Our captain keeps us informed on the nogress with meaningful announcements like "We are now waiting for immediate departure." I wonder what we were waiting for before?

Picture Tammy Baker in a stewardess's uniform. Now picture her make-up tray. The former served what looked like the latter for dinner. Hmm, what's this label on the side? "If swallowed, do not induce vomiting. Call a mortician immediately."

We arrive in L.A. the wrong side of 4 a.m. T.O. time. Rain slaps the pavement, palm trees and cold night air. We are without sleep, and within a few hours, will be riding around California on motorcycles, the envy of everyone back at the office. Is the logic absent here or am I just moving too fast to see it?

Note: Regarding mention of Gary Wolf, at the time I wrote this column he was the man behind Wolf Headers, and also a clever inventor and keen motorcyclist. Wolf Headers is no more, though Gary is still around inventing stuff.
—Max

Excerpts from the notes of a dazed traveller: Part II

June 1989

California has a lot to offer the Canuck fleeing from cold storage: Disneyland, movie stars, mass murderers, traffic jams thicker than home-made marmalade and, tah-dah, the best motorcycling roads in the world.

Continued journalistic mayhem and other marvels that spawn from cramming too much into too little. With no time for naps.
—Max

Away from the cities and expressways, Bruce Reeve and I continually marvel at and revel in the quality of California's paved two-laners. Like small boys on Christmas morning, we greet each new highway like the discovery of a new present under the tree—another mystery treat to be unwrapped.

Smooth, plentiful, and free of frost heaves, the roads snake through canyons and slither along the edges of mountains, coiling back on to themselves. Eternally twisting and tossing, our path climbs, then falls, shakes and gets back

up again. Sometimes we ride for kilometres with only the slightest hint of a straight stretch of pavement. This way tight, that way tight, the bikes bank and bob like sparrows in the wind.

And every few minutes brings another once-in-a-lifetime photo opportunity. The vistas are astounding: never ending, ever dazzling and alluring. Even in the desert, nature's best is on display. Yet, we stop far too infrequently to check out the views, for we are on official business—testing motorcycles in California.

Our path is not without hazards. Often a mere 15 cm of dirt separates pavement from a 300-600 metre sheer drop as the trail cavorts among the mountains. Bruce aptly describes the state as towering mounds of kitty-litter. The terrain crumbles to the touch, and dirt-plows patrol the highways like snow-plows do back home.

Once in a while, a black arrow doing aerobics on a diamond-yellow dance floor warns of extra-tight turns; the recommended speeds serve as a good guideline once doubled. Other fun notices include IMPASSABLE WHEN WET, CHAINS MAY BE REQUIRED AT ANY TIME and IT IS UNLAWFUL TO THROW SNOWBALLS AT CARS OR OCCUPANTS.

During the weekend photo session, a steady stream of cars and trucks hastily descend Hwy 33, each set on delivering a roof-mounted snowman, snow-packed antenna, hood, or pickup bed to the bottom of the mountain before the snow melts or flings off into the kitty-litter. This is no laughing matter. We witnessed one dude emptying a hand gun into the poor snowman that had failed to remain on his truck roof.

Traffic during the week isn't a problem, and we ride fast; the vistas and views flirt with our senses as our eyes race ahead around corners searching for the line and hazards. Gravel, rocks, sand and ice are frequent threats, with only mountain cliffs, the ocean and blue space lying ready to catch us if we flounder. Often, we ride above the snowline, sometimes with a metre of Canadian gold plowed up at the edge of the road. The pace is addictive, exhilarating, a rush so high that any attempt to capture it would only fall flat on the page.

It's not all joy though. California also has restaurants where people line up and pay exorbitant prices for gluttonous portions of petro-barf you wouldn't serve to a starving cat. L.A. abounds in scheduled-for-demolition "luxury" hotels and rip-off rental car agencies all linked to the airport by "shuttle bus service" which is in truth only a clapped-out Dodge van that sags like old ladies' nylons, moves about as fast, and is piloted by some nervous illegal immigrant struggling to see over the steering wheel. And sometimes, it rains there.

It can be a friendly place too, aside from the occasional schoolyard slaughter or freeway shootout. For a few days, we stay at Johnny Carson's old house. Danny Coe lives there now with a floating menagerie of bike racers and friends, and three dogs, only two of which attack me (the dogs that is). We eat his food, use his hot water, dirty his towels and even break into his house because all our stuff is inside and the front door is double-locked so the one key won't work and our plane is leaving real soon.

Moments after busting the hell out of the Johnny Carson signature garage door, we open the front door from the inside to see a surprised and newly arrived Danny standing outside, his now inoperative automatic garage door opener in hand. Getting him to accept compensation for our intrusion proves even more difficult than my first B&E in years.

Packed up, we race to the expressway. The equivalent of Canada's population lives within 160 km of Danny. Right now, they are all out driving, heading for the airport.

Splitting lanes on a motorcycle is legal in California. Doing the same in a Lincoln Continental is not, so we while away the time playing space invaders with this rental scow's electronic what-nots. We had tried for less expensive transport but the minimal inventory of "as advertised" cheapos were long gone, leaving us with the Lincoln or walk option. I wonder whose budget they named the company after?

We red-eye back to Toronto via AA (Airlines Anonymous), avoiding something called "a hot meal" for health reasons. With about two hours sleep to my credit, I arrive only a few minutes late for a Saturday's work at Central Command where I'm warmly welcomed with a list of "must writes," due before Monday. Goodbye Fantasyland.

Singular qualities of dual-purpose motorcycles

July 1989

The world is saturated with compromise. Take big city life, please. The market value of souls on metaphorical Bay Street is pretty depressed these days, but hey, that's where the bucks are, right? The jobs, the action—from a night at the opera to getting mugged on the way home, there's always something going on. A compacted populace suffers the armpit pollution of public transit; the rudely rich flaunt their ill-gotten gains before the perishable clutching their bag-wealth while draped in the latest in Sally Ann couture—why, anyone can see the attraction.

Not that there isn't plenty happening in the country too, it's just that the action there is a little more subtle. It lacks the crowds, pollution, hyper pace and dollar potential.

Another popular Around the Bend theme strikes—some bikes can just do it all. If you have yet to experience the pleasures of a dual-purpose (dual-sport) motorcycle, do it now. Tomorrows don't come with any guarantees.
—Max

The spread of urban life is unavoidable, especially in 200-watt chunks. Unfortunately, what forms an inseparable part of the city fabric often degrades to an offensive, unwelcome intrusion in the country.

I guess one could argue that humanity falls into the latter category. Hiking, canoeing—even those sacred pursuits perceived to be environmentally healthy leave their imprint on nature, the size of that imprint being more attributable to the attitude of the invader than the method of invasion.

I ride in the bush a lot. More times than I can remember, I have come over a rise to catch a deer, moose, or bear munching on some tasty shrub; the animals caught neither scent nor sound of me until I was almost near enough to count the nose hairs. Once, pal Paul stopped in front of me and pointed to an owl. It took me 10 minutes to spot the huge bird in the autumn foliage, but it took the owl at least another five to spot me. I've watched blue herons wing-brake for tree-top landings a few metres away, accompanied a baffled partridge down a narrow trail, and seen beavers build dams at my feet. All this from the seat of a dual-purpose motorcycle.

A good DP bike (not to be confused with the recent run of tarted-up poseurs) is an ideal country companion. Yet, few seem to care. Street riders turn their noses up at the DP because of its dirt orientation. Dirt riders do likewise because of its street orientation. Hiker and canoe freaks turn their noses up at anything that isn't either solar powered or a Volvo or Toyota Tercel wagon festooned with BABY ON BOARD stickers. Their loss, I figure.

One of the oft-heard criticisms hurled at the DP is that it's a compromise. Proponents of this philosophy are missing the point of the machine, ignorant of its true capabilities and the pleasures it provides.

Yesterday, I rode my own abuser-friendly DP from the house, out along the paved road that dances around the flow of the Wistiwasing River, then headed east along the south shore of Lake Nosbonsing. The tarmac ended just before the public beach. Both the paved and gravel sections were riddled with frost heaves. Winter sand still lay deep in the corners.

When I got to Kitten Mink Lake, I turned south down an abandoned tote road to investigate a 40-acre parcel of land that was for sale. The narrow path twisted through the bush, with fallen trees and mudholes strategically placed by nature. Further in, the trail climbed 15 feet up the bedrock along the shoreline and cambered toward the water. It couldn't have been more than four feet wide at best, with the occasional washout thrown in for variety. When the trail eased down to water's edge, I stopped, shut the bike off, and listened to the silence of early spring. I was the only representative from humanity present.

No other single-purpose vehicle could have taken me from my house to the edge of Kitten Mink Lake. Sand-covered pavement, frost heaves, tangled country roads rolled out on marble-gravel or soft, wet dirt—all the white-knuckle stuff for normal street bikes—were a hoot to traverse on the DP, as were the logs and mud of the trail and the tarmac. So where's the compromise?

A street bike wouldn't have done it. A dirt bike or ATV wouldn't have done it either because both lack proper street credentials. A 4x4 truck would have been too wide and too heavy. Sneakers could have managed I suppose, assuming I had a couple of extra days to spare for the walk and didn't mind the blisters and shoe-sucking mud. Meanwhile, my DP wasn't even breathing hard.

Another thing I like about the DP is that it's quiet. That's why I so often catch the animal world napping. It's cheap to own, and street-legal tires allow one to tread over mother nature without plowing knobby-furrows through her terrain.

Sitting on my DP so far north of the 20th century, alone with the spring breeze wafting over Kitten Mink Lake and me, the dual-purpose motorcycle seems like the furthest thing from compromise possible. It's a rare breed.

Maybe that's why so few pay it any mind.

In search of the ultimate garage sale, sort of

September/October 1989

For some reason or other which escapes me, I've been smitten by the compulsion to buy a new house. Not brand-subdivision-new—my body couldn't take the immersion in formaldehyde fumes—but someplace new to me and the entourage. Aside from providing a great excuse for a ride in the country, this quest for a replacement homestead has also been a good learning experience for the local real-estate agents.

Agents don't understand the importance of a garage, or its true place in the domestic scheme of things. They seem to think a garage need only be big enough to hold a car or two. Can you imagine? Putting a car in a garage? Next thing you know, they'll be wanting to put the house in there too. Houses and cars belong

Peculiar, isn't it, how everything you do seems to relate back to motorcycles when you're a keen rider. And peculiar, too, how those who don't ride are unlikely to understand this phenomenon. Hey, I'm not even sure I understand.
—Max

outside. That's why both have roofs to keep the rain off, windows that open and close, and doors that lock so no one can steal them.

Yet they persist in rating this vital structure's capacity as a one-car garage, or a two-car garage. Who cares? That's just as ludicrous as rating it in square feet. How many people do you know with square feet? And why would they want to put them in a garage anyway?

So I set them straight, pronto. The minimum requirement calls for a garage to shelter a modest collection, say five or six bikes. Also mandatory is sufficient space for parts (present and future), boots and helmets; a work area big enough for a proper work-stand and the requisite elbow room to scatter tools about; space for a wood stove, work bench, refrigerator and a parts-wash basin; and the reception area, which should accommodate the unsolicited advice of at least three or four friends. Naturally all this should be situated on the lot to allow for easy expansion.

Only after an agent is educated to these garage realities do I begin to look at houses. At least 45 minutes per handyman's special is allotted to this task. I look at the attic, scrabble around in the crawl space or basement, get out my official Swiss army knife and start poking for rot, mildew, UFFI, alligators, termites and terrorists. Plumbing, electrics, roof–I give it all the complete twice over. And if in doubt, I bring in an expert for another over. The agents hate me.

I have it on reliable account that the average time buyers spend examining a new home is eight minutes–barely time to take inventory of the bedrooms let alone check for termites. A house is not simply a box to park your body and clothes in, it's an infrastructure of interdependent engineering systems crucial to a family's welfare. It is also the single largest investment most people are likely to make. All checked out in a scant eight minutes?

Now compare that to the last time you bought a bike. I'll bet you arrived at the dealer fully armed with road test trivia from every sample of stapled paper claiming to be a motorcycle magazine, the advertised prices from every metropolis within 600 km riding distance, and after dumping all these months of accumulated garbage on to the salesthing, spent the next three hours sitting on the bike of your dreams making appropriate noises.

A bike is a purchase of passion, yet we analyse and rationalize the action to near death, when in reality all that's really important is "will the bike do what I want and am I going to have fun doing it?"

A house is something that protects us. It is at once a place of privacy and a place to congregate, every month of every year. Generally, we keep houses a lot longer than bikes. A house is stability. Yet most people don't spend enough time looking at their new one to notice if it has a furnace.

The solution to this dilemma is to create some meaningless trivia for house hunters to latch on to as bikers have. Houses, and not just the prices (talk about unreal estate) will become acceptable party banter. Soon, real data will slip into the bull bucket, and buyers will approach house buying with the awareness it deserves.

To get things off to a roaring start, I would like to suggest quarter-mile times for houses, projected, of course. This is not as ridiculous as it may sound. A few years ago in Florida, it was proved that police radar units were not above clocking parked trees at above-legal speeds, so surely modern technology wouldn't be at all hard pressed to make the jump to house quarter-mile times. And what more meaningless bit of sacred data could there be? It's the ultimate enthusiast fertilizer.

Magazines like *House & Occupant*, *Chateau Canada* and *Canadian Bungalower* would print an endless stream of pertinent poop for potential purchasers. The eight-minute inspection would be dead. It would take weeks, maybe even months to buy a house. The free world would know what a garage is really for. And real estate agents would hate me even more.

Which is okay, I figure, after what they put me through. Two months of looking and I have yet to find a suitable garage. To paraphrase Groucho Marx, I wouldn't own any house that I can afford. So maybe I'll just get a new bike instead. At least at the bike shop they know what a garage is for.

Note: My solution to the above problem was to buy a hobby farm blessed with a small cottage, small barn and a few outbuildings, and then begin building my own house. With an attached garage of proper dimensions. Thirteen years later, I'm still building the house. But at least there's a place to park the bikes.
—Max

Thanks for the free ride, we needed that

November/December 1989

I was taking a break, chewing on a concoction of chemicals that boasted of a best-before-date somewhere into the next century (it was free, eh?), when a guy walked up to me, shook my hand and said "Thanks." By then, I had almost become accustomed to this frequent show of gratitude, but was never quite comfortable with it. It just seemed odd that anyone should be so appreciative of the chance to ride a new motorcycle, an act once understood as the God-given right of any potential purchaser.

During the '80s, that right low-sided into the slime oozing out of a legal system whose sense of justice had succumbed to greed, while the insurance industry (whose rapacity was never doubted to begin with) responded with a fabricated "crisis,"

This column brings back many fond memories of a very successful program that I had the pleasure of developing and implementing while I was at Honda. When that issue of Cycle Canada hit my desk, you can be sure that everyone from the President of Honda Canada down had a copy of the article.
—Scott Murray

Thanks in part to Scott's lead and persistence, the motorcycle industy—in Canada at least—has come to realize that one of the best ways to encourage riding is to invite people to ride. Nothing like a whetted appetite to stir the hunger.
—Max

levying outrageous premiums to insure any activity associated with any degree of risk. That slime all but strangled a society born out of risk; a society that once prospered on risk. But before we get too depressed thinking about it, let me drop this aside and tell you about Scott Murray. Scott works at Honda, in motorcycle sales—the title doesn't matter except maybe to him and his mom. What does matter is his unwavering belief that *demonstration* is the way to sell motorcycles. Scott is the father of Honda's "Come Ride With Us" program.

The program brought a van load of Honda's '89 street bikes to participating dealers across Canada. The public was then invited to try them out over a prescribed course, with one or two extras tagging along as guides to make sure everybody behaved themselves and found their way back to the dealer. More than 160 such events took place, and of prime significance, about 12,000 test rides were recorded.

The single largest event in Canada, 196 rides in all, took place not in the self-styled centre of the universe, Toronto, but at North Bay Cycle in northern Ontario. My friend Marv and I were there as ride captains, alternating between pole position and back of the grid for each run. All day long, we rode somebody else's bikes, using somebody else's gas, and were sincerely thanked for it by everybody. How could we lose?

Actually, the only people who lost were those who missed the event. Even the most conservative among returning riders spontaneously spewed out comments like "What a rush!" and "Gee, it really is a motorcycle," the latter in reference to the good ship Gold Wing. Certainly the Wing and the CB-1 were the two big surprises of the ride. Nobody expected the CB-1 to be so smooth or fast and nobody, from experienced touring riders to neophytes, ever dreamed a bike as big as the new Wing could handle so well.

A couple of other bikes, like the PCB800, weren't real favourites, but the salient point is that Honda let the people decide and most were very vocal in their appreciation.

One of the goals of the program was to get ex-riders back in the saddle again. "We wanted to get people reacquainted with motorcycles," says Murray. "The bikes are much better now." But the program's underlying aim, part of a larger three- to four-year plan, is to rebuild the motorcycle market. Murray says that this will come from a consistent effort exerted by both dealers and manufacturers, the two working in concert as partners. Hey, Gorbachev and his pet *perestroika* has got nothing on this dude when it comes to radical reform. "I'm really proud of what we're doing," he adds. "We're sure trying, given the restraints."

What restraints? A limited budget in a declining market for one. And the formidable obstacle of lawsuit lawyers and exorbitant insurance rates... There were times when Murray's enthusiasm was probably the only thing that kept his idea alive.

Was it worth it? Honda thinks so. It's already launched the full '90 CR motocross line at tracks across Canada, allowing virtually any rider with the right equipment to try a few laps on the latest Honda racers. Unbelievable. In the coming year, it will be possible to participate in two separate ride programs, one patterned after the '89 run for street bikes, and another for Honda's non-motocross dirt bikes and ATVs, an event which Scott promises will be a family-oriented picnic. There's some other stuff I can't tell you about right now, but it all has to do with getting people back on to bikes, especially, but not necessarily, Hondas.

When I sat under the Honda medium-top at North Bay Cycle, munching on the product of an ingredients list longer than my monthly phone bill, there was no question that Honda's ride program was worth every effort. It was great to see people getting excited about riding motorcycles again. So let me pass on all the gratitude that I was the innocent and largely undeserving recipient of to you and your crew, Scott. Gosh knows, you earned it.

Note: This was my last column for seven years. Not that any mouthy writer can keep his or her keyboard quiet for that long, other topics and venues helping to fill the void.
—Max

Measuring up to memory

January 1998

It's always great to have a new motorcycle company around, but I must confess a problem with the Triumph reincarnate. It started 35 years ago. It was a warm spring day, the sun in full bloom, the snow receding, though a thick layer of ice still remained on the lake. A group of early teens—maybe half-a-dozen—aimlessly strolled the edges of the street's tarmac, pitching roadside stones into the open mouths of culverts. We were occupied in deep, profound debate. Who among us had ridden the fastest on a motorcycle? (Although of pre-license vintage, we were not without experience, having ridden BSA Bantams and a 125 James around the local scrambles track.)

Then, a sound—at once familiar and beautiful—froze conversation.

Although not a conscious decision at the time, in retrospect it seems very appropriate that my return to Around the Bend should involve a story linked to Triumph's return to manufacturing motorcycles. Great to be back, for the both of us. This is a story of roots.

—Max

Around the corner, in the distance, two old guys—maybe late teens or early 20s—were attempting to push-start a Triumph Bonneville. One guy pushed while the other rode, the rider letting out the clutch when the puffed pusher huffed the Triumph up to sufficient speed, and *BRAAAAAA-HERRRrr*, the Bonnie fired and died. This sequence was repeated at least twice—the two guys switching roles each time—as we experts approached at a cool saunter, excitement carefully hidden.

Bump and run
Huff and Puff seemed only too happy to pause for a breath and tell us their story. They had been out for the first ride of the season, noticed the still frozen lake and thought, why not? The Triumph answered that question by falling and subsequently refusing to run for more than a few seconds at a time. Naturally, we offered the benefit of our vast experience, which they enthusiastically accepted. After all, the more help pushing, the better.

What happened next was to alter my world forever. One of the pushers—I can't remember whether it was Huff or Puff—realized that we, being smaller, were probably lighter than they. And that they, being bigger, were therefore stronger.

Thus, didn't it make sense that one of us should ride the bike?

Never before or since have I moved so fast. Seated on the Bonnie, I cracked the throttle wide open as the bike was stirred into motion by desperation and jealous anger (depending on whether talking about Huff and Puff or my once-close friends). Soon, Bonnie and I were rolling down the tarmac about as fast as I had ridden either the Bantam or James. On command, I let out the clutch; the Triumph fired and handlebars pulled ferociously on my arms and tappets clattered and I saw every deity known to humanity and then some and *BRAAAAAAHERRRrr*. The Bonnie died.

The bike rolled to a muted stop. I remained in the saddle, dazed, my hands still clinging tenaciously to the grips. Puff—I think he was the bike's owner—jogged up, breaking my trance with a polite suggestion to release the throttle. A faint clunk in the Amal carburetors added an exclamation point to the Bonnie's silence.

It was just as well hope failed. If it had not, I would have ridden on with throttle pegged wide open until the bike ran out of gas or into something more solid than a mechanical glitch. But, for a blink, I had bathed in the sound and fury of acceleration. It filled my veins, saturating my senses. A mere few seconds, barely measurable in a lifespan. Yet that brief, overpowering elation became the high by which all other events in my life were judged. So you can imagine my disappointment the first time I got laid.

Memory bank
Since my affair with that Bonnie, I have had the privilege of riding some extremely fast motorcycles. For instance, I sampled the pleasure's of a world-championship-winning Ducati Superbike on a race track in Italy, once managed a 10-second quarter-mile, and have ridden over 250 km/h on the street. All major highs. But how can any of them be expected to compete with the power of remembrance, even if old Triumph is no match for new? Obviously, this is a hell of a thing to burden a new motorcycle company with. What can I say? Passion knows no logic.

In the intervening years, as time did what it does, that initial encounter with the mistress of rapid acceleration—while still around, somewhere—became misplaced in my mind's dusty archives. Then, just like that, it suddenly spills out, like the contents of a lost folder when searching through a file-cabinet looking for something else. Careening down a twisted, gravel road, bounding out of a bumpy corner, the bike beneath me sliding under fierce acceleration—*ah hah!*—I recaptured that cherished moment, re-savouring the giddy exhilaration of a forgotten spring day. Granted, it's never as good as the first time, but now it was all *BRAAAAAAH*, without the *ERRRrr*. Coincidentally, this sensual reunion occurred on a new Triumph, the T509 Speed Triple. Not that I intend to jump on an old Bonnie and crack open the throttle—no point in messing up a good memory with the bitter taste of reality—but it's great to have a new motorcycle company around.

Note: With this column, the format for Around the Bend changed slightly from its initial incarnation, Bruce Reeve opting for shorter titles and adding two subtitles where he thought appropriate. Those editors do like to keep busy, you know.
—*Max*

Scratch for dough, deep-fried

February 1998

Saturday morning, around 10 o'clock, we meet

at the bike shop. Have done for years; expect to for years more. Sometimes there's more than a dozen of us, sometimes less, checking out the new arrivals on the showroom floor before heading across the road to the doughnut shop. This second shop-stop—a dedicated non-smoking emporium of franchised coffee and sweets—is a relatively new addition to our weekly ritual. And what a boon it has been to group solidarity, with our numbers (and waistlines) seeming to grow every week.

Perhaps humanity requires this weekly hit of sugar and caffeine, for shortly after we arrive another group keen on growth and solidarity files in for their own fix. Break

Max reminds me that motorcycling has to be fun, because like he says "If it's not, screw it, it's just not worth doing." In this column, Max gave me everything I'm a Burns reader for—wit, sarcasm, irreverence, memorable characters (this time folks I know) and a familiar venue revisited.
—Cheap Ex-neighbour Dave

A column about friends, which in retrospect may be the biggest attraction of motorcycling for what good is a motorcycle without a rider?
—Max

time for the Jehovah's Witnesses, that order of devout door-knockers. En masse, we and they religiously congregate at the counter of the holy doughnut, ordering crullers for Christ and dutchies for the Devil—they dressed as encyclopedia salespeople and we as if it's wash day and all the good stuff is out on the line. Then, with cups and calories in hand, these two disparate factions stake out their turf, the sanctimonious sitting over there, the rowdy over here, mere tables apart, each group absorbed in its own animated conversations.

If you were rude enough to eavesdrop, as I have been, you might hear their side say something like "Hey, did you notice the size of the knockers on that door!" Surprisingly, we, too, make casual comment about the size of recently sighted knockers. They talk about what neighbourhood to blitz next, we talk about where to ride next. Not a great deal of difference so far, just technicalities.

Hold everything! This is Mike Harris country. Shouldn't our two assemblies be talking amalgamation? United, we could become a mega-annoyance. And, bonus, our clan already has some biblically named members, such as Peter and Paul and Chuck. What's that? No Chuck in the Bible? Well there you go, already we're learning something.

Instant losers

Granted, amalgamating can be even more problematic than regular mating. Take our group lottery ticket, please. It's one of those scratch-and-lose things, allowing you to know instantly what an ass you are for spending any money on such an insidious form of government taxation. Wisely, our religious pals have slammed the door on gambling. We can't. Every Saturday, a ticket is produced, its cost divided by the number in attendance. Although no one is required to participate, suppose the one time you decide to get smart and spend your pittance on a double-chocolate sour-cream blob of deep-fried dough, the ticket's a winner? Imagine yourself sitting in the doughnut shop as everyone else runs back across the road to the other shop to buy a new bike. It's almost enough to make you join the nearest cult. So every week, each of us coughs up the price of sin as one delegate scratches the crud from the ticket to reveal–Try Again! *Bonne Chance!* Get Stuffed! *Etouffez-vous!*

During the past two years, we've got our money back twice. Once we even won 10 bucks, which we divided up as one might do with a few fish and crusts of bread among the multitudes. But maybe this week we'll win big.

Man is an island
We have to win; Peter needs the money. Peter Sheppard's a very competitive vintage road racer, which of course means he's perpetually broke. But that's not why he buys into the ticket. This year, Peter wants to fulfill a childhood dream—to race the Isle of Man. It's his last chance. Later this year, he turns 60, at which point, IoM race rules cut him off. (I understand his lady is considering a similar tactic, but that's another story.) So we need to win. It's Peter's ticket to the races (and new bikes for the rest of us).

Actually, I'm surprised some publicity conscious enterprise hasn't stepped in to sponsor what is sure to be a once-in-a-Peter's-lifetime opportunity. Think of the exposure, the name of an appropriate product emblazed across the back of Peter's leathers—Geritol, Metamucil, the local retirement home—as the old geezer crosses the finish line, me busy taking notes. (Didn't I mention that part?)

Hold everything (again)! What about our prospective partners, the door-knockers? Peter's going to need a pit crew. And they could knock on helmets as each racer rides into the pits to re-fuel. "Hello. Have you ever considered how inadequate your present religion is in the event of a crash?" It's a whole new audience.

Okay, so maybe Peter's better off pinning his hopes on the lottery. Dollars for doughnuts, the door worshippers would want him to join them to go door knocking for converts to go door knocking for converts to go... Nice to have a goal, I guess.

Peter's goal for 1997 is to race the Isle of Man. Should the management for Geritol et al want to cash in on this amazing marketing opportunity, they can reach us care of the doughnut shop across the road from the bike shop, any Saturday, mid-morning. We're the ones scratching the ticket.

*Note: Mike Harris was the premier of Ontario at the time I wrote this column. He remains one of the very few people I actually despise, and will remain so until one of us kicks the bucket. Over to you Mikey...
(Keen readers will recognize that the above sentiments have previously appeared on page 41, only in reference to Brian Mulroney, which is okay as these two politicians are as similar as two turds in the same toilet.)*
—Max

Avoid risk at your peril

April 1998

A warm, spring sun found pal Paul and I looking for a good excuse to take the day off, which we figured most likely lay hidden down a nearby USE AT YOUR OWN RISK forest-access road. We were out on our dirt bikes, aimlessly dawdling along, the leaves barely in bud, the blackflies still grounded. The road cut a long, gravel crescent through the bush from paved secondary highway to paved township road, the northwest end being the fun section, tossing and leaping about as if searching for a concealed emergency exit when the theatre's on fire.

To the wonder of no one present, what began as a relaxed outing soon escalated into a full-tilt, take-no-prisoners battle for cosmic supremacy. For miles, Paul and I charged through the corners,

I was launched into motorcycling via a relationship. At the end of that relationship I was questioning why and how I would stay in motorcycling—I had no friends, acquaintances or family who rode, and I knew very little about bikes. For over two years I didn't tell my father I had a bike—his father was killed on a bike. My father came for a visit and as I explained it to him, I also managed to sort out my how's and why's. I copied this article and asked my Dad to read it and then read it again. Thanks.
—Kelly Cornford, grande dame of the Blackfly motorcycle endurance rally.

It's particularly gratifying for me when my words strike an important chord with a reader. Makes it all worthwhile.
—Max

throttles pegged to the stops, XL and XR just a breath apart, sometimes even touching. For miles, handlebars thrashed back and forth as humanity and machines slid and bounced a mere heartbeat from oblivion, none willing to give an inch. And for miles, under the helmets, behind the goggles, Paul and I both grinned and giggled as we flirted with death and dismemberment. This wasn't mere foolish horseplay, mind you, it was important, a thing that mattered, a race of honour to see who could get back to the trailer first.

Midway through a corner–I don't recall which–during a sudden slither–'scuse me Paul–a stray insight dusted its way into my helmet. That USE AT YOUR OWN RISK sign is in the wrong place. Rather than at the entrance to the forest-access road, it should be posted at the entrance to life, or at least at the entrance to adolescence.

Sissy stuff
Exposure to risk is an inescapable part of life. More than that, it's a primeval need that to date evolution hasn't managed to wean from our systems. Yet where evolution has failed, humanity itself is close to succeeding. Increasingly, we are becoming a society of sissies. Sure, we still want to take risks–to go mountain climbing, deep-sea diving, white-water rafting–just as long as it doesn't involve any chance of injury or loss. After all, jeopardy is just a game show on TV.

So a person takes a risk, an accident happens, a person gets hurt. Could happen to anyone, right? Except the person who got hurt. Rare is it that the aggrieved pause to consider whether the incident was a result of their own desire, or even need, to push the limits. Somebody else must be found at fault, and if somebody can't be, then blame it on El Niño. Either way, somebody else must pay.

Misplaced fault is particularly pitiful when the hurt or loss involves loved ones. How do you tell grieving parents that the main reason their kid's now impersonating a potted flower is because they failed to ensure the child had proper instruction, had proper equipment, or was even made aware of any risk? You don't. And overcome by disbelief, anger, and tears, they sue. Anyone; everyone. Psychologists call this transference of guilt. Lawyers call it a windfall. Insurance companies call it an excuse to increase premiums. I call it bawling for dollars. Isn't there any onus on humanity to assume some responsibility for its own actions? Not even vegetables are entitled to a risk-free existence.

Speaking of which, years ago a few conservative acquaintances (they seem to have all forsaken me over time) claimed I was harbouring a secret death wish. They would point to the speed, the fast cars, the motorcycles, and anything else that set off their danger alarms, like old guitar strings that could snap in the night. As usual, that clichéd death wish was being confused with a life wish. If anything, life could use more USE AT YOUR OWN RISK options.

Couch victims
Given the choice, is it not better to die living than to remain living dead? The land of the living dead occupies the crypt in front of the TV, spits out the end of a narcotic needle, pours out the neck of a booze bottle, hides in the countless pages of over-regulation—basically lurks anywhere we subjugate our freedom in exchange for a pre-programmed existence, preferably with guaranteed minimal risk. Yet by seeking to eliminate risk, we unavoidably eliminate much of what makes breathing such a worthwhile enterprise.

Obviously it's safer to simply sit back and watch. But so what? Where's the advantage of being the last one buried if your spirit died years before you? When it comes to life, use at your own risk, and use often. Climb a mountain, hang-glide, bungee-jump, go out on a date. Or, to quote the Parry Sound Sportbike Rally's perennial hard-luck winner Phil, "Ride fast and take chances." But whatever you decide to do, make it your own choice and accept the consequences, be they success or failure. After all, you won't have the chance once you're dead or, worse, self-assigned to the comatose couch of the living dead.

As an aside, I won that race with Paul.

Upload this, sunshine

May 1998

Late Sunday I'm typing away as letters chisel out across the fuzzy-white screen of my computer monitor, the letters quickly building into words, the words gradually revealing how Archimedes' ancient musings relate to the centre of gravity of a volume of displaced water–an amusing ditty to be sure–when I decide to quit for the night. That's when it dawns on me, though I don't know how things can dawn at night. No matter, computers more powerful than the one now processing these words are beginning to appear on motorcycles. Not that my computer is a worthy example of leading-edge technology, but it's a scary thought.

I'm not one of those Neander-tools who mutter in lament of the loss of motorcycle technology so

Anyone who relies on a computer, particularly when it constitutes an integral part of one's profession, will inevitably fall into a sordid and consuming love/hate relationship with this cursed bitch of bits and bytes. Thus trapped, this column reflects my frustration with the course of technology.
–Max

primitive anyone could fix it with the toolkit Aunt Ethel gave me for my fifth birthday. Frankly, I don't want to work on the damn things; I just want to ride 'em fast and irritate other road users. No, what really worries me is that eventually–and it's bound to happen–the philosophy of computer technology is going to download into motorcycles. Yes, all those bits and bytes currently calculating mathematical relationships between air temperature, atmospheric pressure, intake-manifold vacuum, fuel flow, throttle opening, and maybe the rider's inappropriate use of corporate logos, are soon going to behave more like the computer right here on my desk. This frightens me.

Known bugs
For one thing, computers are distrustful and argumentative. Picture this: you're on the latest whizbang motorcycle, rapidly speeding toward an infraction of the law, when Bowser the dog bounds out directly in front of you. *Grab the brakes!* and a small screen just below the instrument panel lights up: "Are you sure you want to stop? Yes or No?" Of course I want to stop! Why the hell else do you think I grabbed the brakes? Finger exercise?

Unfortunately the computer doesn't believe you and before you can click the "Yes" button, you crash. "Application error on part number AH995500. Do you wish to reboot? Yes or No?"

Another thing that bugs me about computers is bugs. Most programs provide some sort of text file, there for the new purchaser to read after the program has been installed on his or her computer. Typically, this file lists all the reasons why the program won't work on his or her computer, reasons that, for some reason, the company neglected to mention prior to purchase or installation of said program. Often this list is titled "Known Bugs."

These are the bugs the programmers know about, the tip of the infection-berg. So, having taken delivery of your new WhizbangRRR (the Rs are the salesperson laughing while walking away with your cash), you turn the key and there, on that small screen just below the instrument panel, is the list: "Known Bugs."

• Warm days may cause overheating.
• When ridden in the rain, left turns may cause electrical system to malfunction.
• Right turns are not yet possible with this model.
• Failure to check oil level prior to starting engine may cause...

AROUND THE BEND (AGAIN)

Damn, the engine just died. Anyway, a quick call to the help line ($1.50/min) tells you that a fix is in the works, WhizbangRRR Ver 6.2, this upgrade to be available late December, with special pricing if purchased before yesterday. You mean I have to pay to get my bike to work as well as it was supposed to when I bought it? And wait until next winter?

High-tech marriage
The enemy has landed. And it's downloading into all facets of society. Next time you get married (Spouse Ver 9.3, with all the hottest features—nice body, a job, good credit rating and a truck), you crawl into bed, snuggle up to your sweetie, and are handed a flashlight with the list: "Known Bugs."

• Snores.
• Unauthorized advances may cause system to lock up, leading to hard-drive failure.
• Birth-control devices not included in this version.
• Virus checker not working.

So this is what they meant by bed bugs. Of course, it's quite possible the "Yes" button will fall readily to hand as love conquers all, only to be confronted by "Do you really want to exit? Yes or No?"

Anyway, back to the important stuff–bikes. Truth be known, the concept of having to pay to make your new bike perform as advertised is not new. At one time, if enough customers made enough noise about some fault, the manufacturer would issue a recall, an expensive and embarrassing procedure.

But computer-think doesn't even try to make things work–just wrap the product in advertising and then sell 'em an upgrade. With all new bugs. And true to our past, we will eagerly buy into this corporate con job.

Honestly, it's depressing enough to make me want to run off and join the Canadian army. So there I am, in the heat of battle, when the sergeant bellows: "Attack!" Instantly, I respond. "Are you sure you want to attack? Yes or No?"

The philosophy of computer technology has won the war.

Your ticket to their profits

July 1998

It's a legal fundamental that once a lawbreaker has paid his or her debt to society, the person is absolved from further prosecution and persecution. In fact, Canada's Charter of Rights and Freedoms, Section 11(h), states that any person charged with an offence has the right, "if finally found guilty and punished for the offence, not to be tried or punished for it again." Mass murderers, child molesters, the low vermin who derive great pleasure in torturing their victims, every transgressor who has ever been found guilty of an offence are by law free to continue their lives without further fines or imprisonment once having paid that "debt." With one exception.

There is a crime so heinous, so vile, that governments permit

It enrages me that insurance companies continue to penalize me even after I have paid my penalty, fine, or done time. I have paid my penance; insurance companies don't have the right to continue to rape my wallet, but they do.
—Michelle Duff, retired motorcycle GP racer, author of "Make Haste Slowly," and the world's fastest grandmother.

Why is it that when governments get into bed with the insurance industry it's always the general populace who gets screwed?
—Max

public punishment and persecution of the offenders years after the crime has occurred and their "debt to society" paid. This villainous act? Exceeding the speed limits of our roadways.

Floggings all around
Never mind the debate as to whether speed limits make any sense beyond a source for government revenue. You speed, you get a ticket, you pay your fine and maybe even serve a jail sentence. Then, for the following three to five years, you continue to pay as the punishment carries on, this financial flogging often dispensed by private enterprise, any charter of rights or sense of fairness be damned. To facilitate this breach of justice, governments willingly open their books to the insurance industry, typically providing computer access to confidential driving records.

All this so the same insurer can continue to castigate you for—and profit from—a violation of law where all judicial claims against you have long since been settled. The rationale for this trampling of individual rights is that speeding poses an additional risk to the insurer.

Bunk. Speed has never been shown to cause accidents. Rather, it is a person's inability to operate a vehicle at a certain speed in certain conditions that causes accidents.

Many of us are quite capable of safely operating a vehicle above posted limits. Many others are not capable of safely operating a vehicle at those same speeds, or even at speeds below posted limits. So if risk is an acceptable excuse for continued prosecution, then why not go after those who pose the risk rather than those who know how to operate a vehicle safely?

But suppose we ignore that line of logic. And suppose too that you got caught shoplifting today. I know it's unlikely—you're too good at it—but say you got nabbed just this once. Or better yet, maybe twice or even three times. Unlike speeding tickets, frequency doesn't matter, for at no time is any shop owner permitted to charge a convicted shoplifter more for the store's product than the price set for other customers. Nor can the shop owner demand to examine anyone's criminal record prior to selling that person the shop's wares. Not even the aggrieved shop owner, the one you ripped off and the only one to suffer a financial loss from your wrongdoing.

The law is clear on this, even though shoplifting does increase a merchant's costs, which must in turn be either absorbed or passed on to the public. Yet insurance companies are allowed this privilege, encouraged even to take full advantage of it, this despite the fact that, unlike the above merchant, insurance companies suffer no financial loss from the dubious crime of speeding. Truth is, the only loss suffered from speeding is by the offender found guilty, and that's strictly from the fines and ensuing persecution by the insurance industry.

Innocent, as in uncaught
For the record, at the time of this writing I don't have any speeding tickets. In fact, I haven't been charged with any infraction of traffic laws, anywhere in the world, during the past 25 years. (I'm sure insurance companies will all be crowding around computer terminals downloading government records to verify this claim, which of course gives me even greater pleasure in being able to proclaim it.) So it's not some personal vendetta or questionable driver's record that prompts this tirade.

What irks me is two things: the inane focus on the velocity of the vehicle rather than concentrating on the competence of its operator; and the abdication by governments of their moral and constitutional responsibility for law, enforcement, and punishment. If exceeding speed limits—which were established years ago when neither roads nor vehicles were as safe as they are now—is a bona fide crime, why do governments so readily subcontract partial rights of punishment to the only commercial enterprise that stands to benefit financially from the public's continued transgressions? It is, after all, the insurance industry, and not any elected government, that establishes the appropriate degree of punishment for the crime and then collects on the punishment to fill its own coffers.

Obviously, if there exists an unpaid debt to society, it is with the insurance industry and not the alleged outlaws found guilty of breaking a crime of such spurious legitimacy.

You go this way, I'll go that way

September/October 1998

This may not come as much of a revelation to those who know me, but a large part of my life has been guided—subconsciously or otherwise—by a simple credo I call Max's Maxim, which states, "If everybody is going that way, then there's good reason to go the other."

Obviously, the route resulting from this maxim rarely proves the easiest or speediest way to get from point A to point B, but then, that is the point, isn't it? In life, destination *should* take a back seat to route. Contrary to popular myth, all roads don't lead to Rome, or even McDonald's. But all roads do eventually lead somewhere, even if it's only to a dead-end where you can stop to pee before doing an about face back to the last crossroads. So why fuss about destination?

Here, my personal philosophy gets tossed into the car-versus-motorcycle debate along with a few thoughts about destination-fixation. You're only here once; why not enjoy the ride?
—Max

Destinations only become important when the route chosen to get there is a drag (which is usually the case when destination takes precedence over route). So where does this all lead? Cars versus motorcycles, sort of.

Take the car, please
Normally I'm not the sort of person to stir up controversy, but have you ever considered taking the car instead of the bike? Never mind the well-advertised advantages of automobiling—roof, doors, windows that roll down and then back up again, air-conditioning to keep you cool, a heater to keep you warm, room for the dog and groceries, safer if you hit a moose—the principal difference between car and bike is that the car, at least for me, is usually quicker. Not faster, but quicker.

For example, if I have to travel to the Megashity (or Megacity or whatever the heck it is they're calling Toronto these days), there's about 350 km of due-south major pavement between reality and Lalaland (I'll let you decide which end is which). So I get in the car and about three and a bit hours later I'm there queuing up for an exit ramp on some clogged expressway, at which point I turn on the car's tape deck and tune out to tunes. Now, on my bike, I haven't got a tape deck. But then I wouldn't have reached that ramp yet, either. I would have exited a long time ago, seeking the pleasures of some empty backroad. Max's Maxim in action.

Indeed, I have been known to go to great lengths, in distance and endeavour, to avoid where everybody else is going, or has already got to. Granted, this goes against one of the primeval urges of humanity, which is to congregate. Humans are naturally drawn to each other, which can be a good thing should you fancy a certain other member's members, but unfortunately it doesn't stop there. Clusters gather to form communities, which attract ever increasing numbers until village grows into city, somehow along the way managing to jam-pack everything distasteful about humanity into the smallest space possible. And to escape this mayhem—something humans paradoxically all seem to want to do—the inhabitants all head to the same vacation spots and attractions, typically on the same weekend. This, of course, not only crowds the destinations, but most of the main routes that lead there.

So how do you avoid such destination-driven crowding? It may seem a contradiction, but one way is to use a map. Although maps were designed to get you where you're going—destination-oriented, in other words—they can just as easily lead you away. The trick is to look at the roads, not the places they connect. Check out what a road does, what it might take you through—the terrain; the backroad communities strung together by family farms and the scent of manure. Maps reveal roads as yet to be ridden and small villages that slow you down to PLEASE WATCH FOR OUR CHILDREN, with ma-and-pa dinners serving an out-of-fashion combo of good food and honesty. These are roads that wander into the land rather than simply carry travellers up and over it. These are not car roads. These are motorcycle roads. And invariably a good motorcycle road takes you longer to get there.

Time machine
Obviously, we don't always have the luxury of time. Sometimes, we have to get some place right now, like yesterday. Then, I take the car. And even if I'm not in a rush, I'll often opt for four wheels over two if the route is a drag. If the trip is unavoidably boring, why compromise the experience? It's like getting undressed to read the *Globe and Mail*—it won't make the experience any more enjoyable.

True, there are fun cars available if you live by the credo that money conquers all. But there are no boring motorcycles, at any price. So most of the car candidates for my driveway may be pleasant perhaps, but boring. Most are also cheaper to operate than the majority of bikes I crave. Which just goes to prove that economics is boring too.

So a car is practical and efficient. And boring. As is most destination-oriented travel. The final destination, after all, is death, a place nobody seems to want to go but eventually we all get to. And if you haven't enjoyed the ride there, there's no second chances. Which is why I prefer to seek out the backroads on my way.

Escape goats and other excuses

November/December 1998

Three and a half weeks. We just dropped everything and left. It was the longest Jackie and I had been away from home since we decided to partner our various sets of dinnerware, towels, sheets, and leftover Xmas cards some 25 years ago. BMW prepared a K1200RS in Vancouver for us, and we rode it fast, trying to find the slowest way back home to northern Ontario. We followed an undisciplined route charted mostly by caprice, searching for mountains, bumping into forgotten prairie towns, pausing to record the happenings at Sportbike West, all good fun, all of which you can read about later. Assuming some editor or publisher doesn't kill me first.

You see, when I got home there was this mountain of mail sitting on my desk—not quite as high as the

Work should never interfere with life. It's a philosophy I chose to follow many years ago, a philosophy I only I waver from when the bank account gets perilously low and the usual scrimping won't help.
—Max

Rockies, mind you, but certainly a rival to any bulge on the Prairies. And my computer was nervously byting its bits wondering how it was supposed to cope with all the accumulated e-mail.

First mad rush came via my book, *Cottage Water Systems*. Apparently, the distributor had—without forewarning—sold out of the second printing. Normally this wouldn't be such a big deal—just print another batch—but the publisher was screaming for an update of one chapter which had to be done right away because the stores were all sold out and the selling season was upon us and blah, blah, blah.

Money talks
At the same time *Cottage Life* magazine wanted me to write a big feature for big money. In keeping with industry standards, this too was needed right now. Badly. Must have.

Not to be out-done, the publisher of my soon to be released book titled *The Dock Manual* had finally finished the second draft of the edited manuscript, its 80,000 or so words now needing to be re-read and approved by me. Immediately. And apparently the art director was "getting nervous" about not having received my approvals for the artwork. And what about the photos? Leaves are falling from the trees and the snow will soon be upon us; who's looking after the photos? And there were the notes and photos and finances of our wonderful western swing to sort out.

Just to add a personal note to the mounting mayhem, our well went dry. First time ever. And me, the author of a book about rural-based water systems. Just further proof of nature's dry sense of humour. Fortunately, about the only well in the area that hadn't gone dry was Cheap Neighbour Dave's. So we could at least bum a bath, just in case you were worried about catching some bug while reading this. Anyway, I attacked Mt. Madness in my usual methodical manner, loading up the rifle just in case the fortress was attacked by angry editors, and let's see, need to get those photos of docks fast before the weather changes. I started to organize a photo shoot, getting addresses and photographer lined up when—what? You can't be serious. Suddenly (again), the book's publisher wanted every owner of each photographed dock to sign a release form. Ridiculous—the owners already said I could take the flippin' photos. I phoned the publisher, a U.S.-based company—which at least explains some of the paranoia. The editor explained the rest.

Sheepishly, she revealed how the publisher was once sued by a goat. Seems the picture of said goat appeared in one of their books. The owner of the goat then sued on behalf of the goat, claiming damages for the trauma the goat suffered as a result of having its picture taken and subsequently published. Kid you not. The goat and the publisher settled out of court for a lot of bucks. Certainly heartening for the animal rights movement, but what if I couldn't get those signatures? Maybe I could sue the goat...

Max walks
Then Bruce Reeve called. He had four motorcycles lined up for the annual *Cycle Canada* slow food/fast riding fall tour. Was I in? Life's perpetual balance teetered before me. On one side of the balance, hectic work, the completion of which would certainly give our travel-beleaguered bank account a substantial boast. On the other side, stuffing myself silly with good food, riding vacant backroads draped in autumn colours, all at somebody else's expense, all in the company of three good friends.

I grabbed my helmet and headed out the door.

Funny, but when I returned five days later, all the work that had threatened to collapse desk and computer was still there, still waiting to be done, piled even higher, actually, with more frantic notes from editors and publishers even more stressed out than before. Instinctively, I knew exactly what to do.

When I arose from my nap, yet another editorial nag roosted upon Desktop Mountain–it was half-past this month's column due time. Lost for words, I went over to Cheap Neighbour Dave's and watched an advancing storm light up the night sky while we ate chips under the roof of his porch. And the next morning, water reappeared in our well.

As I explained to my editors, it's simply a matter of establishing priorities.

Here's a prize for you

January 1999

Another year, another scourge of awards. You know the routine—whatever of the year, gold here, best of this there, pat on the back. Yet never so much as a "Well done, chum" from the folks at *Cycle Canada*. To rectify this oversight, I hereby submit my pick of the pretty darn good, a few of the recent highs of motorcycling that came to me while fighting a bad cold.

But first, to the important issue of nomenclature. Seems self-evident—because of the origins—that these coveted and highly sought after laurels should be known as the MAX awards. But Bar Hodgson of International Motorcycle Super-Show fame already scooped MAX (Motorcycle Awards of Excellence—bit of a stretch) for the awards he hands out at his hotsy-totsy January

Despite my previous condemnations of merit awards in general, I offer this very subjective praise for a few of the peripherals of motorcycling.
—Max

show. Not that I'm bitter, but he could have at least asked. So robbed of that opportunity, I have decided to call mine BAR, short for Burns' Awards of Recognition.

Takes a licking
In no particular order of merit, first BAR goes to the General Electric Rough Service Lamp, 100 watt (the only item here I had to pay for). This is a real bright-idea bulb for anyone reduced to working on their own motorcycles, whether out of economic necessity or masochism. (There's other reasons?) Down in the barn, wrenching on my bummed-out Beemer, with trouble lamp dangling from a nail driven into the rafters, a foot catches the cord and *thwack*, trouble lamp tumbles to the floor. But something's amiss; the light's still working. Impressed, I re-hook the lamp to nail, and *thwack*, immediately do a repeat. Obviously I'm no candidate for an award here, but some sturdy light bulb, eh? Normally, I would have been up to the house to forage for another, which would have soon shattered too among the cliché cascade of curses. But this GE gem keeps on shining, twice thwacked. No trouble lamp should be without one.

Continuing with this enlightened theme, BAR two goes to the Wolf BMW key-fob, acquired free as part of the goodies handed out to everybody at Sportbike '98 in Parry Sound. At first glance, it looks like a useless bit of ad-trash. However, back at the barn, my Beemer won't fit through the door with luggage attached. Not a problem in daylight, but at night, trying to insert a tiny luggage key into a tiny hole, neither of which is visible in the dark... grrrr. Now, I have seen the light. Not a lot of it, mind you, the whimper of red illumination from the Wolf fob just reaches its intended target (no threat of anyone mistaking our barn for the local house of ill repute). Still, it's enough luminance to do the job. And later, I pull the same trick at the front door of the house. Award worthy, yes, yet perfection has escaped this device. For instance, all the promo Wolf paid major money to have printed on this teeny torch has since rubbed off from the abusive action in my pants' pocket. And sometimes, while pocketed, the switch gets accidentally bumped and the light goes on. This causes a faint, red glow to appear next to the groin, leading countless young ladies to inquire "Hey, is that a Wolf key-fob in your pocket or are you here for a good time?" Well, both actually. Unfortunately, the glow fades as parts wear, so somebody should talk to GE about getting a Rough Service version. Of the key-fob, that is.

A catalogue of entertainment

BAR three. I have trouble with the concept of paying for catalogues. Why spend money to view products a merchant is begging me to purchase? Here's the only good reason I've yet to discover: The Rider Warehouse Catalog. Never mind the bad spelling, this gem is chock-full of motorcycle-related goodies—riding suits, fancy boots, luggage, camping gear, electronic gizmos galore—all first class, no junk; all great drool fodder. Of course, this alone does not make it BAR worthy. What elevates this catalogue above the rest is its entertainment value. It's a grand read, well worth the buck and a bit Cdn, even if I did get mine for nothing. For instance, scattered throughout the issue I scored (new one rumoured to be in the works) are fictitious items such as the "Least Direct Route Navigator" and "Loud Pipes Save Lives Cassette Tape." Conversely, some of the genuine merchandise maybe should be fictitious. Try a temp/humidity pen for $47 U.S. Who needs this? But just below that bit of electronic uselessness is something everyone should have—fake oil pools in three different sizes, looks like the real thing, place 'em under a friend's bike (preferably just after a major rebuild). Quality bungees (surprise, they exist!); T-shirts emblazed with "Cars Suck," "Pave The Planet" (my fave), and the like; maps and map holders; handlebar clip compasses; and on and esoteric on. Well written, amusing, lavishly illustrated—a highly recommended couch-potato activity.

Final BAR of the season goes to Bar Hodgson, not because he lets me into his show for free or once gave me a MAX award—both acts of obvious and considerable merit—but because he let me ride his Wassel trials bike. I've never ridden a worse motorcycle. So while it's good to recognize the highs, it's also good to know where the bottom starts.

One-upmanship for two

March 1999

Bruce Reeve's editorial of last month greeted the new year with an interesting potpourri of put-downs for passenger carrying. Certainly his heated remarks regarding bicycles were hard to fault but when his tirade over-boiled onto motorcycles, my support cooled. Some of my more memorable and thrilling rides on a motorcycle have been in the companionship of a passenger. Jackie, specifically.

Jackie began motorcycling as a rider, not passenger. She has owned sportbikes and dirt bikes and ridden a number of *Cycle Canada* test bikes. She rode to work, and together we travelled as a duet–she on her mount, I on mine–covering many miles over the years. In the twisty bits I would blast off up

The seeds that sow each Around the Bend blow across my desk from all directions. Even with the window shut. This one blew in from a column Bruce Reeve, Cycle Canada's editor, wrote.
–Max

ahead, then slow down on the straights until she caught up (this happening increasingly less as the shared miles accumulated). Then, a few years ago, she decided to sell her bikes and become a passenger.

Pillion power
There's no question that any motorcycle operates better one-up—including all those tour-ships bragging of pillion welcome mats and the like. The one-up motorcycle accelerates quicker, handles better, stops faster, is less influenced by crosswinds—cripes, it even consumes less fuel. But the real problem with two-up motorcycling is the control a passenger can exert on the bike—consciously or otherwise—almost always a result of inexperience.

Bruce describes rookie passengers who flail about the back of the bike like a pendulum, yet whose fault is it? How is a neophyte to know what to do without instruction? Fact is, no passenger gets on the back of my bike without being told how to behave, their experience be damned. With my ass on the line as much as theirs, it's do as I say or walk. Yet typically, some nincompoop rider will treat the neophyte passenger to a blast of wheelies, peg-scraping lean angles, hard acceleration, and flat-out speed runs, then loudly lament that the mate won't ride with them anymore. Duh.

Granted, there are times when lugging around a bunch of ballast out back can dampen the thrill, much like throwing cold water on two dogs caught in an amorous moment. The cold water doesn't stop them, it just makes everybody grumpy. So sometimes I prefer to ride alone. Fortunately, Jackie not only understands this, she knows when I vote to go solo she wouldn't enjoy the ride anyway. Yet on so many more occasions, the riding experience is so much the better for her attendance.

For one thing, having a navigator on board can be a real bonus. I also stop more often when carting a passenger, which isn't a bad thing. And because the public seems less intimidated by motorcyclists touring as mates, strangers are more apt to say hi. Even when riding off-road, a passenger can be handy, dismounting to test the depth of those murky, blackwater holes ahead. Should the hole prove too deep, at least the bike's still safe.

As to why Jackie opted for pillion position, she lists "time to think, to watch the scenery, and to daydream. And there's no pressure to stay up on two wheels—that's the rider's problem." Obviously a passenger must have a great deal of faith in the operator, something

Bruce considers a folly. So I guess the next time he flies to Australia for a new bike launch, he'll be piloting his own plane. Point is, if you're worried about the operator's ability, don't get on board, no matter what the conveyance. Fortunately for both Jackie and me, the "excitement of the speed" is also one of the reasons she enjoys being my passenger. Yet had speed been part of her first ride on pillion, there probably wouldn't have been a second. Jackie's the only person with whom I ride fast because she's an excellent passenger and, contrary to past editorial assertions, to be a good passenger requires talent. For one thing, it takes a great deal of skill to do nothing when everything in your body screams that you are about to die. And also contrary to popular myth, it helps to have riding experience.

The rib-poke

So when Jackie and I are cookin', the front tire pushing out in the corners, with bits underneath paying the odd visit to the pavement, she doesn't fret. She knows from her own riding experience that anything she does out back can have just as serious a consequence as anything I might do up front. We ride as a team, a fine example of interdependence at work. Granted, once in a while I get the proverbial rib-poke, not because the speed itself is problem, but usually because there's some scenery that requires a slower pace to fully appreciate. At least from the passenger's point of view. Being a team, we slow down a tad. The other thing I've come to enjoy about riding with a passenger is the intimacy–that unspoken communication and requisite physical closeness. For me, this has become an increasingly pleasurable part of motorcycling.

Recently, Jackie expressed an interest in riding again, to have her own bike for day jaunts–as a duo and on her own. No surprise, really, for no matter how good it might be out back, it's still no match for front-row centre. On this much, Bruce and I agree.

Mandatory and predatory

April 1999

Spring is a celebration. It begins as cold and snow recede, every day a watchful sun climbing higher in the sky. Birds court, sailors scrub down hulls, and motorcyclists dust off bikes for that first ride of the year. And, just the other side of Neddow's place, Bill's getting ready for a bath. Spring, you see, melts the ice off the creek out back.

Perhaps it's no surprise, but Bill's a bachelor. And—no shock again—twice he's been abducted by flying saucers. Yet what Bill and I have most in common is that we both own a tractor. So for us, spring also means removing chains, snowthrower or plough, and going for that first unchained ride of the year.

On the road running adjacent to my property, a tractor is the

Increasingly, government-mandated regulations are choking the air we breath and stifling the freedoms we claim to love. Is humanity really that stupid that it needs, and usually demands, instruction and policing for everything it does? Seems to be the case.

In this column, the case for freedom is made with my tractor, coincidentally a Case.

—Max

only motorized vehicle a person can legally operate unburdened by mandatory helmets, seatbelts, insurance, vehicle license, proof of ownership, or even vehicle safety standards. Travelling flat-out along that road, sitting high with hair blown straight back by a southern breeze, I am bathed in a wondrous feeling of freedom. So what if flat-out barely squeezes past 30 mph? A tractor is not a vehicle for doing things quickly, but for doing things methodically. At speeds that on any other vehicle would bore the likes of a cow, a tractor entertains. And everybody nods or waves as you pass on by. Not just the owners of the same make of tractor, or even just fellow tractorists, but the whole shootin' match—kids, grandmas, folks in the back of pickups, folks in cars, folks raking away the last vestiges of winter, and the odd motorcyclist. Even the cows nod. In fact, it's possible that there's no friendlier place from which to view the world than a tractor. Any work done in the process is a bonus. So who cares that a tractor dispenses velocity and handling about on par with a douche bag? If I want speed and handling, I'll take the bike.

Your profits, my misfortune
To take a motorcycle on the road running adjacent to my property, I have to fork over an annual licence fee, money theoretically earmarked for road maintenance but instead gets absorbed into that great trough from which politicians scoop out their hefty pensions. And I have to insure the bike at ridiculous rates because, in Ontario, my insurer is required to pay for any potential personal damages that might result from some imaginary schmuck hypothetically smacking into me. There's even a mandatory life-insurance component attached to the policy, which has more to do with mandatory profits than vehicle insurance. And the bike has to meet an increasingly bizarre list of vehicle regulations. And I have to wear a helmet, even though it's my head I'm putting at risk. Hey, if the dolts responsible for this stuff are that worried about me having an accident, maybe they should be the ones donning helmets just in case it's one of them I take out (at least we can hope).

The tractor needs no such paperwork—it's mine because I own it—and therefore contributes nothing to any lard-ass political retirement fund. And though the insurance industry would go into orgasmic delight if political dupes legislated that everything—right down to the teeth on the fleas on my dog—resulted in fat premiums being deposited into its bulging pockets, so far my tractor has remained out of their greedy clutch. As for vehicle regulations, all the tractor needs is a "slow moving vehicle" red triangle attached to its hind end. This is no big deal—something that would also benefit most vintage motorcycles. Harleys, too. In fact, according to Ontario law I don't even need a horn, though I do have one. Ariel, my granddaughter, demands it.

Tractor facts
My tractor's a mid-'50s Case 410. Start it up and listen to the idle; the engine turns over almost slow enough to count the revs. Redline is around 2,000 rpm, lower than most motorcycle engines begin to make power. Besides the foot throttle, there's a hand throttle—the original cruise control—that allows me to set the pace a chug or two below walking speed. With no suspension, you don't want to go a whole lot faster through the fields. So is it any wonder Bill's only vehicle is a tractor?

Of course, all is not perfect in tractordom. Parts prices, for instance, are staggering, high enough to make even motorcycle parts seem a bargain in comparison. And it's not often a tractor operator is moved to stop, jump off, stamp both feet on the ground and yell *yahoo!* immediately after passing through a particularly fine bit of twisty road, as I have done when riding a motorcycle. No, a tractor doesn't get much adrenaline flowing—more inclined to slow it down to a trickle. Which isn't a bad thing at times. At such a peaceful pace, with no helmet to interfere with ambient sounds, you can hear the birds flirting above the engine's low rumble. And, if you were driving past Bill's farm, you might also hear the splash of bath water. Assuming you happened to be out on your tractor that day.

More likely, I would be blasting by Bill's place on the bike, somewhat sideways, just a siftin' her with Neddow or Paul. Such highs don't come cheap, but they always seem worth it that first ride in the spring.

Just try to wiggle out of this

June 1999

Toes don't get much attention. On the other hand, fingers are into everything—rude gestures, squeezing brake and clutch levers, reaming out nostrils—all manner of necessities. But toes? Mostly ignored. So I never gave mine any thought. Not even when sprawled across Dr. Doug's office floor, my innovative choreography and cursing the culmination of eight years of gathering pain. Even Dr. Doug ignored my toes. He was focused on the CAT scan of my back.

"Oh wow, is that ever big!" he said excitedly, reviewing the scan of my lower-most disc. According to Dr. Doug, that delinquent disc dramatically bulged out beyond vertebrae on all sides. "I've never seen one that bad." Dr. Doug gets excited about anomalies of human design.

While there remains some debate whether the six degrees of separation theory holds true for connectivity between humans, there's no doubt that it applies to connectivity between keen motorcyclists and their motorcycles. For some of us, almost everything seems to relate to that lowly two-wheeled societal annoyance.
—Max

However, unable to walk, stand, or sit, I failed to embrace his enthusiasm for anatomical deficiencies.

Reluctantly, he drew himself away from scans of spinal curio to consider my reparative options. I could camp out in bed downing handfuls of nasty, potentially addictive drugs gambling that my spine might restore itself over the next three months or so. Apparently, such miracles happen, though not usually for discs as dilapidated as mine. Or I could be hacked open, a repair attempted, and stitched back up. This too works for some people. When it doesn't, next step is to recut and then fuse the two lower vertebrae together. So let's see, Door One, opt for the bed-and-drugs plan and I might still need to go under the knife. Or Door Two, surgery, which could lead to multiple intrusions and a potential loss of mobility. And of course—the good doctor tossed out as a cheery afterthought—mistakes do happen. Rare, he attempted to assuage my concerns, but not unheard of. Bit like miracles. So it's possible a botched slice and dice could leave me paralyzed from the waist down.

Pick a door
Slithering around Dr. Doug's office floor, I commented that his menu of remedial measures sucked. And further, that his office ceiling tiles were truly ugly. This aside, it became obvious that my best hope for recovery lay not on the floor or ceiling but behind Door Two. The way I figured it, by the time OHIP (Oppressive Harris' Insurance Postponement) found a vacant hospital bed, sufficient time might have elapsed for a miracle to occur, thereby allowing me to take a pass on the slice-and-dice. If not, nothing lost eh?

It was back home wasting away in waiting, vegetating between Star Wars sheets while snacking on painkillers reputedly strong enough to cause an elephant to forget, that I remembered my toes. Know what they're good for? Wiggling. Suddenly I realized that in the event of a "rare" surgical screw-up, I could be robbed of this simple pleasure. And hence, the much greater pleasure of motorcycling. Granted, this would take a supreme butcher-blunder, but what of a wee slip of the knife, leaving toes partially wiggly? This little piggy went to market, this little piggy stayed home along with the rest of them. It was an unwelcome thought that lay next to me, breathing uneasily like last night's impromptu date, reviewing last night's impulsive promises, as last night's fiery encounter unravelled with daylight. What to do, what to do?

Call for the Vette

Depends on the degree of "from the waist down" damage. For example, suppose the only disability was erectile dysfunction. Evidence shows that the most likely consequence of such an affliction is an inexplicable urge to rush out and lease a Corvette which, though no match for a motorcycle, apparently seems to do the trick even if the afflicted can't. But what if one leg completely crapped out–a lump of limb to be dressed everyday for a role of no use. Just like a senator only without all the perks. Not an agreeable prospect. Still, I reminded myself, I once rode with an acquaintance whose right leg had been amputated, his bike only slightly modified to accommodate his injury. Together, the two of us rode fast and with no loss of fun. And don't dismiss the much-maligned sidecar. Jackie and I toured Brazil and Oregon by sidecar and I have since toyed with owning a hack. Not quite a motorcycle, but still a hoot to ride. Yet what if a slip of the scalpel left me paralyzed from the waist down? A few brave souls steer electric wheelchairs onto flatbed-style sidecars. But could I tolerate the endless insensitive questions such as–"What happened?" and "What's it like to drive?" To me, the operators of these contraptions may best illustrate the devotion and passion that drives motorcycling. But could I match their courage, even if it were my only option?

All this from toes. Who would have guessed the misshapen little appendages could hold such heavy thoughts? Then, when the call came from the hospital, all wondering of wiggles was pushed aside.

Post-op, captive in a cage of hospital bed, anaesthesia slowly retreating into consciousness as eyelids lethargically awaken, I focus fuzzy attention on toes. This little piggy goes to market, and *look!* They're all going. Get me my motorcycle! These toes deserve a ride.

Bituminous bump and grind

July 1999

For me, one of life's greatest highs hits when riding silly-fast down an unfamiliar backroad, a twisted wreck of a road, its course surveyed by madness, its surface a mess of potholes and heaved pavement all iced in sand and gravel. Attacking a blind crest, a snap calculation from the treeline suggests the path veers right when—oh golly—road jags sharply left, decorated in dusty debris, bike slides, both tires screaming for traction. And there, in that fleeting instant, dancing at the edge of death and destruction's welcome mat, only the deft play of throttle, body positioning, and delicate use of steering inputs separates potentially painful failure from triumphant, exhilarating success. Some folks climb moun-

Here's a subject that's near and dear to my heart—improving riding skills. Although only one riding school of my preferred type is mentioned in the column, I have since become aware of several around North America. Find one close to you and sign up, even if you've never ridden a motorcycle before.
—Max

tains, I like to scale backroads; I'm not the only one who gets a kick out of tempting fate.

Losing your grip
In truth, my reprehensible backroad behaviour is rarely exercised (one reason I'm still around to tell about it, I suppose). Typically, I don't set out to ride silly, it just happens when the moon and stars line up with my mood, the day and the road. Oddly, the type of bike doesn't matter–two wheels and a motor will do. And should nothing line up from a cosmic perspective, I still refuse to shy away from one of those seductive backroads, for even at a nearer-to-sane pace there's too much fun to ignore.

So I'm always surprised when confronted by an intolerance, and even fear, of rough road. Go to a motorcycle rally, visit a website, eavesdrop on a conversation at a biker cafe, and guaranteed you will eventually encounter some rider whining leather knickers into a knot over a bit of bituminous bump and grind. Toss in that most evil of road rascals–the unpaved pathway–and it all conspires to stare down the average street rider into a quaking mass of apprehension. Admittedly, most street bikes–sportbikes in particular–are happiest on smooth pavement. But Canadian realities don't allow for smooth curvaceous pavement to happen often or for very long. In this harsh climate of frequent freeze-thaw cycles, nature refuses to be smooth-talked into cooperating. So many of the country's best motorcycling roads have bumps. And sand in the corners. And spectacular scenery. But that's life in a nutshell, ain't it? Even the best of it has the occasional rough spot.

Perhaps the biggest stumbling block to rough-road enjoyment is the dread of sliding. The bike hits a smear of sand, bike slides, rider panics, bike and rider crash, and the road gets the blame. Another blacklisted beauty. Yet the only time a sliding bike should be a problem is when it's on its side. Any other time–whether on pavement or hard-packed dirt–below that sprinkling of sand and gravel lies traction. A rider only need find it, and avoid crashing while in the process of looking. (Gravel on gravel, where traction perpetually rolls away under skinny motorcycle tires, remains my personal nemesis, but I'm working on that one too.) Once a rider discovers that sliding is not only okay, but often the fastest and safest way around a corner gone begging for traction, those once-dicey backroads turn into a glorious playground.

Into the bush

Not that I'm telling anyone how to ride—just how to learn. When it comes to upgrading street-riding skills, the majority of keen motorcyclists lean in the direction of track schools, either of the high-performance street-riding type or race schools. While it's true that participating in as many of these as you can afford will undoubtedly improve riding skills, it's also unlikely any will turn a dedicated pavement rider into a confident backroad charger. Even motocross schools, where bumps and dirt abound, won't do the trick. All these centres for faster learning share one unavoidable fault—each operates under controlled conditions that rarely exist in the unkempt haphazard latticework of Canada's tortured tarmac. In the cruel real world, predetermined braking points and visible apexes—memorized by repetition—a lack of oncoming traffic, even which way the path's headed, all quickly become figments of race track imagination. As does a manicured, predictable road surface.

Serious backroading demands wide margins for error, not scuffed knee pads. Knee draggers invariably end up in the bush. Which, coincidentally, is where they should have started. Only trail riding allows a rider to learn the art of sliding in an atmosphere of real-world surprises, such as ruts, mud, sand, rocks, etc., all at relatively slow speeds. And—speaking from personal experience—dirt is usually softer to fall on than pavement, a bonus best appreciated when lying next to the bike.

While track schools appear to be gaining in number, I know of only one trail-riding school—a priced-right gem started by Blair Sharpless and Warren Thaxter, now run by Steve Weykamp. Popularly, it's known as the Trail Tours and Dirt Bike School (officially, try Ganaraska Off-Road Motorcycle Adventures; 705-277-9511), an easy commute from Toronto. It's also one of the safest ways to enhance street-riding skills and backroad giggles.

Tempting? Just tell 'em fate sent you.

Passion versus utility

September/October 1999

A movement, caught in the corner of my eye, revealed a tentative step forward, baggy pants easing in my direction. Not the baggies of currently trendy recycled fads, but baggy with a cuff and pressed crease, the way men used to wear pants back in the '40s and '50s. I was leaned over securing luggage onto the bike, preparing for another day's ride to some place, doesn't matter where. I looked up. Not too far above the pants' waistline—which sat about where half the civilized world chooses to wear a bra—was a friendly smile.

"They've sure come a long way," said the smile, words coloured with accent. I reciprocated the smile greeting, which in this situation is invariably interpreted as a sign to continue, which he did. He used to ride in the old country, he said,

Offending readers is not a bad thing. If a writer tries to never offend anyone, he or she invariably offends many folks simply by the banality of the writing. But when I intend no offense, yet offense is still taken, I'm often surprised. Peter, an internet acquaintance, was offended by this column's reference to old folks and I'm not sure why. It does, however, remind me (again) that not everyone gets the same message out of a statement or story. This is good news. It would be a seriously screwed-up world if we all believed what we read or heard, regardless of the source.

Anyway, I liked this column so it's in the book.

—Max

offering time-enhanced memories of speed and adventurous travel. Before they had roads, naturally. Or speed, if memories were bound by truth.

Pop's cycle
This impromptu exchange was not an isolated incident. It happens to me almost every time I'm out on a tour, alone by the bike, some guy (yes, it's strictly a male thing) shuffling over to tell me, in one phrase or another, that they don't make them like they used to, the voice a confused mix of admiration and regret. And now that I think about it, these encounters are more likely to happen when I'm on a sport-touring bike which, with the requisite acres of swooping plastic and integral luggage, perhaps best captures the visual essence of modern high-speed two-wheel travel. Or maybe it's the fact that, with mechanicals hidden by body parts, the bike appears more car-like and therefore less like they used to make them.

Fine, but why doesn't this happen when I'm loading the trunk of the car? My car—fairly basic four-door transportation—boasts enough techno-wizardry to shame almost any motorcycle (okay, so it lacks an ice cooler), yet no one ever saunters up to comment on how "they've come a long way." And when was the last time you had a visitor walk into your living room and make the same observation about your TV? Yet, put a modern motorcycle before them—a bit of technology that has in fact not come as long a way as most cars or any TV—and suddenly they're both surprised and in awe of the apparent technological advances. So what did they expect, acetylene lamps?

Why does this happen with only the motorcycle? Two reasons, by my guess. With cars, TVs, toasters, and the like, we're dealing with utility. Whenever these items change to offer increased utility, so much the better. Everybody's pleased when the toast pops up golden brown, the charm of the old drop-side toaster notwithstanding. And nobody laments the loss of fuzzy 10-inch black-and-white images of Ed Sullivan. But with motorcycles, we're dealing with passion, and passion complicates everything. And when a motorcycle changes to offer increased utility, sometimes passion suffers. Passion is one of those unmeasurable items motorcycle journalists struggle with under the heading of "character." Also, don't-make-'em-like-they-used-to critiques are usually delivered as sudden realizations by gentlemen long removed from the sport. They've sat in their living rooms for decades, watching as the TV upgraded to multi-media home entertainment centre, enjoying every advancement for as long as it took them to get used to it (about a week on average) before looking to upgrade (with no regrets), yet they haven't looked closely at a motorcycle in years. At least until curiosity caused them to wander over to chat while I install luggage.

Retro grade
No wonder what they remember doesn't jive with what currently sits before them, the bikes of their memories being as old as baggy cuffed pants. I can certainly sympathize. I love the beauty of vintage motorcycles, the simplicity, the purpose of line, the sound of barely tamed internal combustion. And I'm very appreciative that so many folks have chosen to restore, display, and operate these gems of the past, giving the rest of us a chance to vicariously enjoy that beauty. Truth be known, with eyes and logic misted by those dreaded time-enhanced memories, I occasionally experience the seductive tug of nostalgia urging me to buy some huffing AJS, Velocette, or other aged and oily jewel. But fortunately I can never seem to get the time-machine kickstarted.

Personally, I'm thrilled and thankful they don't make them like they used to. (And who are "they" anyway?) I relish brakes that rely on more than hope to stop, and reliability that exceeds that of a politician's promise, and horsepower enough to blow the doors off that recently leased Ferrari. But none of this I relate to these smiling strangers in cuffed pants. Usually, I just nod in agreement, often listing the technical virtues of the bike in question—which never fails to impress—and then listen to the stories. Maybe if they talk long enough, they'll think about re-entering the sport. People shouldn't deprive themselves of a passion so easily attainable.

The end is nigh. Maybe

November/December 1999

In the area of Canada I have come to call home, some time after the trees have quit littering the world with variegated, orphaned foliage, leaving only grey skeletal limbs pointing to a grey sober sky, about when the landscape becomes dominated by a drab, damp sombreness—mid-November at the latest—it's time to put the bike away for winter. Every year, it's the same routine, and every year I keep putting it off, using any excuse to hold off for that one final ride.

Last year, I had intended on taking notes, not to describe the procedure of motorcycle storage, but to try to capture the metaphysical perspective—the stirred memories of past rides, the discoveries of neglected maintenance as bits of the

It's never as good as the last time.
—Max

bike are washed and scrubbed with a detailed fervour mustered but once a year. With hands numbed from the cold and wet, only to later sting from the heat of hot oil as it drips past that dastardly drain-plug over fingers, I would take notes. Oh the insights, the spirituality of the occasion, the bidding adieu to a good friend. I even kept the notebook at the ready, waiting for the day. Except, it never happened.

Winter warm-up
Last year, the tailings of autumn lingered as (so we were told) ocean currents off the west coast of South America convinced the snow in mid-Ontario to hold off well past bedtime. So no proverbial blanket of white. Sure, there were days when I knew it had to end, that winter was about to tumble over my driveway. And each time I would reach for my notebook and head for the barn, only to have the sun come out and warm the porch thermometer. Which brings me to December 15th. The week previous had been visited with cloud and sub-zero temperatures, driving frost deep into the earth. But no snow. On the 15th, the sun shone, making it a swell day for that final pre-storage wash of the bike. I stepped outside with bucket in hand and–whoa–a warm blast of air washed over me. Thermometer said 8 degrees Celsius. Brain said let's go riding.

I called Neddow. Neddow lives about 40 minutes southwest of me in an area inhabited by ex-draft dodgers, artisans, commune members, and similar vestiges of peace and love, all severely out of fashion in this decade of soaring stock markets. I, on the other hand, live in an area where most everyone is related, I think. (At least there aren't as many last names to remember.) About half way between incense and incest is a road bookended by a warning: USE AT OWN RISK, ROAD NOT WINTER MAINTAINED. If truth held any power, three other seasons would be added to that sign. No matter, Neddow and I agreed to meet somewhere along that narrow, winding, unpaved path, its postponed maintenance in perfect harmony with the weather, our bikes, and our moods. Work would have to wait for a frosty Friday. We were going for that last ride of the season.

In the shade, traction abounded on the dirty backroads and we rode fast. Where the sun swept the path, frost turned to mush, leaving a slimy layer of mud about half the depth of a tire's sidewall, the road's surface tattooed with truck- and car-track imprints. Charging out of traction into slime, we aimed for a thin lip outlining the ditch, finding virginal turf, a soggy sliver less inclined to steal control of steering in exchange for passage. Following an aimless itinerary, we found ourselves on Bear Mountain, a bit of a topographical exaggeration. But in these parts, folks are accustomed to the making of mountains out of hills (after all, Mike Harris's constituency is just to the north). Still, it did get noticeably colder as altitudes increased. A two-track trail coaxed us into the shade of a pine forest where puddles lay frozen between mounded patches of iced dirt, which added no shortage of variety to our riding styles.

Back on the backroads, we left telltale skid marks around corners, riding until the cold finally caught up with us, and we parted, each back to his own out-of-fashion neighbourhood.

It's a wash
With a red-ball sun shivering on the western horizon, I hastily washed my bike, convinced this would definitely be my last chance. Mud was everywhere, stacked deep on top of carbs, clogged in the swingarm, caked on the motor. I barely had time to hose away the big chunks before the sun disappeared and the bike went back into the barn. The next day, winter arrived. And not long after that, my back crapped out. So I never did store the bike. Or take notes capturing the deep, metaphysical meaning of it all.

But this year, I pledged to do it right. With winter breezes licking at dust under the barn door, the dog and cat chasing barn phantoms, I sat on a milk stool next to my bike, tools and notebook at the ready. I placed a screwdriver under the clip of my Beemer's right-carb float bowl, and then stopped. What if Bing carbs aren't Y2K compatible? And what about my battery charger? Should I be stocking up on volts? And never mind the bike, is the rider compatible? To any K? I stepped outside to think things over. Hmm, a warm breeze. Wonder if Neddow knows anything about Y2K?

Safe at any speed

March 2000

It wasn't the first time I had been accused of "riding too fast." Even this magazine's editor has laid a similar charge. I responded to Mr. Ed by asking him if it had been Mick Doohan—instead of me—on the bike, would he have still considered the bike's pace too fast. From this, Mr. Ed somehow got the impression that I thought I was on the same level as Mick, which wasn't the point—I was just riding my own pace, having fun. Then there was the time I was asked to lead a group of vintage-bike riders on a tour of some treasured roads. They were all experienced riders, yet I still felt obligated to remind them to ride their own pace, assuring them that I would always wait at intersections for the slower guys, and if anyone felt I was

A variety of irritants surfaced here, all from the widely held assumption roughly summed up by "my way is the right way and the only way." Imagine what a fine place this world would be if we all realized there are ways other than our own to go about living. But don't imagine for too long—returning to reality will only depress you.

—Max

riding too slow, let me know and I would fill them in on the route so they could blast ahead. Later, when stopped at an intersection to regroup, the group complained that the pace—close to posted limits—was too fast. Say what? Who's in charge of your bike's throttle? I shrugged and handed the lead over to someone else.

But this time, on hearing the accusation aired again (from someone who had never ridden with me, ironically), I replied, "No, I don't ride too fast. I ride at a comfortable pace for me. If you are uncomfortable trying to keep up, then it's you who are riding too fast, not me. Conversely, if I am travelling slower than you wish to ride, I'm not going too slow—I'm still riding at that same pace suited to my comfort level—it's you who are now riding too slow for your comfort."

Mission control

As soon as the words were out, I realized that in one short paragraph I had summed up my basic philosophy of riding, and perhaps life. I don't do things based on the performance of others, but rather on what I feel interested and capable of doing, continually opting to exercise my right of control. And I'm sure that it's this potential for control that for me constitutes one of the big attractions of motorcycling.

Of all motorized ground-based vehicles, none equals a motorcycle when it comes to allowing the option of control. For instance, most motorcycles still permit a rider to fully preside over braking, choosing not just when and to what degree the braking force should be applied, but also at which end of the vehicle. The amount of lean, and how that lean is initiated—through handlebars, footpegs, knees against the tank, whatever—is all rider initiated. Most other road vehicles don't even ask you to choose gears anymore, which fortunately is still a requirement of riding. So why aren't we celebrating this opportunity to take charge of this one small portion of our lives and assume the responsibility for riding our own bikes?

Perhaps because the notion runs counter to a basic hallmark of humanity—our tendency to judge another's performance based on our own limitations. It's the Goldilocks syndrome—what isn't right for us is wrong for everyone. Nowhere does this manifest itself more blatantly than with that usurped birthright to operate a vehicle on public roads. Once tucked behind our own steering wheel or handlebars, nobody operates a vehicle as well as we do. "Hey, will you look at that nut? Who the hell does he think he is, going that fast?" or "Hey buddy, can you drive a little faster? It's not like I got all day," or "Quit riding my ass, mister; I'm doing ten over, that's plenty fast enough in these conditions."

Righteous road turds
I have a personal hate-on for the slothful slime who dam the flow of traffic, thus forcing long lines of fellow travellers to put lives at risk in order to get by. Yet I know they aren't going too slow, they're simply travelling at a pace comfortable for them. But must these mobile morons be so bloody rude and inconsiderate, lacking the modicum of respect required to pull over to let others pass? A few years ago when touring Washington state, an unusual road sign caught my attention, the frequently repeated sign instructing any vehicle blocking five or more vehicles to pull over and let the traffic pass. There were no exemptions for being on vacation, or piloting a motorhome, or doing posted limits, or even exceeding those limits—if traffic gathers behind, you pull over. Here, the opposite is true. Obstructing traffic has become a duty of the righteous road turds, a sanctimonious band of self-anointed Knights of the King's Highways who, by divine guidance, know the safest speed for today's conditions. For every one of us. And it's their sacred duty to obstruct all sinners attempting to exceed the lowly limits the turds' meagre talents warrant.

This tirade aside, I have acquired an increasing reluctance to ride with riders I don't know, and big groups are definitely out. With my friends, we have a respect and admiration for each other's abilities. None of us ride too fast or too slow; we just ride and enjoy it. And if that enjoyment comes at a faster, or slower, pace than mine, so what? It's their bike; they're in charge; none of us need to be reminded of this.

We just ride our own bike.

Middle-finger discount

April 2000

It came as a revelation. Deep down, I already knew it, but the truth sat stewing in some back closet of my mind, unadmitted, unrecognized. Then with genuine surprise, it dawned on me—I'm a polygamotist.

Yes, I admit it, one bike can never satisfy me. True, I've had several bikes at once in the past but I considered it just a passing fancy; thought I had settled down to a normal monomotous existence. Until it came time to buy a new bike. Then one would no longer do. Suddenly, I needed several.

Sadly, no matter how charming a motorcycle, it can't do everything. I need a bike to ride off-road and one for careening down twisted backroads and one for two-up touring (yes, I'm into that too) and one that looks so

Just another injustice perpetrated by the insurance industry, mixed in with the advantages and pleasures of owning a bunch or two of motorcycles (or bunches of anything that needs insuring, for that matter).
—Max

absolutely stunning that to bitch about its excruciating discomfort seems petty and an ugly one just to ride on shitty days and one that loves sliding on gravel roads, and... You get the idea.

I presume it's like the polygamist with many wives—one to cook great meals, one to look stunning, one to do the gardening, one to clean house—let's see, what else? Oh yeah, typing—you can always use a good typist around the house. Yet, while the life of a polywhatever may sound appealing, obviously there are some corresponding downers. For one thing, initial costs are greater by a factor of how many of whatever it is you want to get poly about. But I can live with that—pay once up front and you're done. Then there's maintenance. Even motorcycles that sit around and do nothing will deteriorate. Ditto for wives, I guess, but I can't say for sure, mine's active (maybe ask your local old-style Mormon). But maintenance keeps things working as close to perfection as possible, so again, this expense I can rationalize. What I do have trouble with are those costs of participation that you have no control over, and that keep repeating, which for polywhatevers can really hurt. For instance, a polygamist must cope with the secondary effects of multiple PMS (that thought alone keeping most men monogamists). And similarly, the polygamotist has to cope with the primary effects of PIS—Penal Insurance Syndrome.

Go forth and multiply

This is one poly-expense that confounds all logic. Say you own six bikes (allowing you to rest on the seventh day). If you want to ride those six, you have to insure all of them. But how many bikes can you ride at the same time? It's not like I'm going to be coming around the mountain riding six white motorcycles when I come.

True, some insurance companies offer multiple-bike discounts. For instance, Canada Life Casualty, the MMIC's insurer of choice, offers a 7 per cent discount for multi-bike clients. Sure, I'll take it, but seriously folks, big bloody deal. They act like they're doing you a favour when in reality the more bikes you have, the more money they make. Multiple bikes typically spend most of their time collecting dust while the insurance industry collects multiple premiums. So the industry increases its income by the number of bikes you own while increasing their exposure to risk by what? Likely less than the 7 per cent or similar crumb discount graciously offered out of the goodness of their collective black hearts. It's a no-brainer–less use equals less risk.

Besides proper vehicles, such as motorcycles and tractors, I also own a truck and a car. The insurance premium for either vehicle is based on driving 20,000 km per year, a distance the two barely top combined. The rest of the time, the four-wheeler fleet sits around in the driveway. So while the insurer's risk is reduced dramatically, all I get is a measly 10 per cent off the cost of mandatory insurance. And because multiple motorcycles are typically used even less, the risk per vehicle reduction to the insurer is even greater.

Unrisky business
One industry defence of this scam is that I might lend a bike to a friend. As a believer in the proverb "never lend your bike or your wife as they'll both come back screwed," it's an unlikely scenario in my case. But suppose you're not so inclined (send picture of wife). Then it's true, the insurance company's risk increases. Yet premiums collected versus risk still remains disproportionately in the insurer's favour as long as the bike collection spends most of the year collecting dust–a truism for every collection I know of. So the defence is bogus.

I'm not suggesting the insurance industry isn't entitled to make a greedy fat profit, or even benefit from my polygamotist leanings, but it doesn't make sense to penalize the customers from whom it stands to gain the most. A reasonable discount–50 per cent say–for additional bikes would encourage polygamotomy, which in turn would put more money into insurance industry coffers, not less.

Meanwhile, because my recent lottery investments haven't worked out as well as anticipated, it's unlikely I will be able to pursue my newly realized true polygamotous self. Gadzooks–that was my second revelation of the year!

Maybe I should ask for a discount.

Note: The insurance company mentioned here has since changed its name (suspicious?), and the MMIC is the organization that purports to represents the Canadian motorcycle industry's best interests.
–Max

Unsafe at home

June 2000

Have you noticed the controversies heating up the Readers Write pages? The criminalization of speeding, whether or not ignoramuses should wear beanie helmets, the dangers of wheelies (particularly for double-standard cops), banning potato guns (or was it bra-less ladies walking through soft-drink warehouses?)—all hot topics to be sure, but it was the suggestion to outlaw "sexual congress while standing up in a bath tub" that caught my attention. The problem, as I discovered, is not with congressing about while standing, but with the tub itself. Turns out this humble bathroom appliance is a serious hazard, especially to motorcyclists.

The discovery happened last Saturday. It was a dandy spring day, the toasty sun ignoring sub-zero

Rarely can you find so many different subjects and opinions squeezed into such a compact space as a magazine's page devoted to readers' responses (at least if the sampling is an honest reflection of received responses, but that's another issue). In celebration of this confusion, this column was initiated by Cycle Canada's eclectic mailbag (Readers Write), and then my computer took it trials riding, somehow finding a link to other favourite Around the Bend themes.
–Max

readings on the outhouse thermometer as warm rays gnawed away at the snow in the fields. And as spirits also warmed, a trials bike came out of the barn. Second kick, the bike started. Following a half dozen or so blasts up and down the front pasture–a required ritual to heat-up the two-stroke internals to the point of comparatively smoke-free combustion (compared to a coal-fired generating plant anyway)–I steered for the play area. With deft precision I bounced over and weaved around old truck tires, railway ties, and rotting logs.

It was a slippery world, the earth touched by a blush of morning frost as motorcycle tires slithered about in quest of iced traction. Slowly, the earth's epidermis began to thaw, adding an additional film of wetness. Still, I continued to conquer all obstacles before me, slipping, sliding, moving sideways as much as forward, confidence re-asserting itself. At least until a crust of log peeled away under the biting tread of a low-pressure tire. The bike fell, taking me with it. (It's always the bike's fault, right?)

Let's try that again
Together, we landed on the log, engine still running, me mentally still riding. Instinctively, I pulled in the clutch lever, picked up the bike, and–no go. The engine and I were keen but nobody told the rear wheel. Looking down, I saw the chain hanging loose, pried askew by a bent chain tensioner. Okay, push the bike back to the barn. With a big screwdriver, I poked and prodded into holes previously bashed through the casing, eventually coaxing the chain onto the front sprocket (proving that crash damage can be beneficial), and then walked the chain onto the rear sprocket. One kick and I was back to conquering humanity's discards.

But the stuff of trials legends (home division)–the steep rock and fallen trees–lurked in the bush, calling. Dripping with confidence, if not perspiration, I accelerated up the back trail. Tapped out, fourth gear, the bike rapidly consumed the hill, its front wheel skimming a damp, thick mat of brown leaves, the perfidious residue of last autumn.

This would translate to about 60 to 70 km/h when I hit the ground, the bike and I continuing as a twosome, uphill, sliding until our mutual ascent was called to halt by a tree stump. The engine raced madly, the rear wheel a keen partner this time as it spun madly against my leg. Feeling less enthusiastic about trials riding than the bike, I reached over and held the kill button down until the commotion ceased. Then I kicked the bike off me. In the ensuing peace, I lay on the hard, frozen ground and wondered why I had not noticed its solid state a few moments earlier.

Roused by the smell of gas, I raised my body and then the bike. The gas line was broken. The throttle housing was broken. Stuff was bent. Again, I pushed the bike back to the barn.

I replaced the split fuel line, wiggled broken pieces of throttle housing into approximate position, straightened the twisted footpeg and brake lever, and one kick, I was fouling air anew. My body was sore—I was sure the fall had bruised a hip and perhaps a rib—but there wasn't enough discomfort to quit riding, so into the field I returned. The stuff of trials legends could wait.

Tubbie terrors
No crashes marred the rest of the ride. Fact is, I just got bolder and bolder. Eventually, with moto-needs temporarily sated, I rode back to the barn and parked the bike.

All in all, I felt pretty darn good. I even said as much to myself as I later eased into the tub to soak (it being Saturday night), the steam of a hot bath seeping up into the air, carrying worries away with it. I reached for the shampoo—*yeeow!*—major pain in the side. Seems a bruise had transformed into a cracked rib.

So (and perhaps you smelled this coming) we need to ban baths. In fact, anyone who insists on bathing should lose their rights to public healthcare. Alternatively, I suppose we could all learn to accept responsibility for our own actions (assuming governments would get the hell out of our unshampooed hair and let us). Sure. Given the option, I suspect most people would prefer to skip baths entirely than face that scary thought. Me, I'm compromising, forsaking bath for shower. Which leads to this puzzler—should the opportunity to congress present itself, should I wear a helmet? Or will a B.C. beanie do?

Pretty new, but not too pretty

September/October 2000

I think I'm having a Twilight Zone moment. I buy a new bike and the phone starts ringing. Okay, so it's not completely new. It's a demo, one of those low-mileage vehicles boasting a modest discount as an incentive to overlook a mysterious past. Worked for me. As for the bike, it's a red one. Or, as Neddow later observed, a '65 Ford Mustang-red one. Anyway, the calls began as soon as I brought it home, starting with Cheap Neighbour Dave. I didn't tell him about my new bike (his wife works for the OPP, so I think his line is tapped). Instead, I hung up and rode across the field to his house (did you expect me to use the road?). Confronted by this uncharacteristic expenditure of mine, Dave circled around the bike in silence, dealing with his shock by busying

Introducing a new bike to friends is nearly as much fun as riding the damn thing. Assuming you can find time between introductions.
—Max

himself picking out sections of young saplings from between the front disc and fork and bits of grass crammed between foot levers and the engine. Soon, the rest of the Cheap family tore themselves away from the TV to come out for a look. David The Younger said "Cool." Jessica The Daughter said "I didn't know BMW made motorcycles." She's blonde.

I told her that my previous bike—which she had seen on numerous occasions—was also a BMW. "Oh," she replied. And that BMW had been making motorcycles since 1923. "Oh," she replied. After a moment's thought she added "Well I think it's too pretty a motorcycle to ride in the dirt."

"No bike is too pretty to ride in the dirt," I corrected her. I never did find out why Dave called.

Long-distance caller
I knew why Peter Hoogeveen was calling. Typically, he only calls when passing through the area looking for a place to sleep one step up from a picnic table or motorcycle tankbag. I told him the barn was booked, my new bike taking up the guest stall. Snagged, he asked "What new bike?" I told about the BMW. "You bugger," he spit out in envy. And him sponsored by Honda. Is there no shame among long-distance riders? If so, they aren't alone. Another out-of-the-blue call—coinciding with the Hoogeveen visit—sent a series of unanswered rings throughout the house. So Hoogeveen answered. On the line was someone who never returns calls, let alone takes the initiative to make one, a non-BMW manufacturer's representative. (Name of the rep being withheld by request of the family who would prefer Dad kept his job.) Although there was a business purpose to the call, at the rep's insistence our conversation was dominated by talk of my new bike (Hoogeveen had spilled the beans). Turns out the rep had just asked his boss for permission to buy one just like it but for some reason (conflict of interest or some such minor matter), his request was denied. Go figure.

Then Gord called. At least this wasn't a surprise. When I told him about the bike, he rattled on enthusiastically—barely a pause for a breath—about the phenomenal gas mileage his BMW club newsletter reported for my bike.

Like, who cares? I in turn told him how stable the bike was at 170 two-up. Yet on my way over to Neddow's, riding one of the No Winter Maintenance forest access roads strategically located between us, the bike running a steady 90 km/h, both tires drifting across the gravel corners, I thought, "You know Max, one of the bike's manuals claims you're getting 85 miles per Imperial gallon while doing this." Yes, there are two owner's manuals. It takes that many to hold all the Cautions! and Warnings! and Attentions! and Notes! inspired by North America's bizarre legal system. Of course, the bike's German, so nothing is simple.

Bored and stroked
Meanwhile back at the phones, Don called. I think it's the second time he has done this. Anyway, concerned friend that he is, he wanted to know how my back was faring. So I told him about the bike, mentioning its top-speed capabilities. He responded in disbelief. "How could that be?" Don's motorcycle mind is stuck in the '50s, though fortunately the rest of his brain has advanced well into the '70s. Or parts of it anyway. Vintage bikers really need to get out more often, which Don probably would if his BSA started on a regular basis.

Prior to sliding my way over to Neddow's, he too had phoned. That's why he already knew about my purchase. Neddow wanted to know the bike's bore and stroke. I searched through the manuals, eventually finding it in the "Service and Technical Booklet." Apparently, it's the same as some Kawasaki, though by BMW's math it's one cc more. All this Neddow knew right off the top of his head. Pressed (and not very hard), he will also recite the bore, stroke, valve-guide diameters, valve sizes, clearances, and a whole lot more you didn't need to know about a 1953 Willys Jeep. Or a flat-head Ford V8. The man's just a wealth of useless information. Like early Mustang colour schemes. And he can work all this into one telephone conversation, which is never a bore with him.

As to the specific model of my new bike, it's a... whoops, gotta run, the phone's ringing again and I think I'm beginning to see red–'65 Ford Mustang red.

Not in the forecast

November/December 2000

Memo to Piero: In retrospect, I should know

better than to listen to the weather bamboozlers. But it was raining when you called, temperature in the single digits. Just as predicted. So it seemed reasonable to put off going for a ride simply for the pleasure of going for a ride. It got even colder on Saturday, a nasty wind blowing in from the north. Sunday brought more grey, thankfully stirred by warmer air. Then grey washed away to white, with patches of blue scoured in between. By noon, blue predominated as great fluffs of white floated around like candy-floss balloons. And the temperature soared into the 20s. So you should have come up.

One of the nice things about living here is that good riding begins just beyond the barn door.

For me, savouring a late-season ride squeezed between batches of bad weather is one of the true joys of motorcycling. Subsequently rubbing that joy into the wounds of a riding partner who opted out due to forecasted bad weather just adds to the pleasure.

–Max

(Earlier this morning there was a mega-moose there too, but that's another story.) We picked a destination—the chip shop in Mattawa, because we hadn't been there this year—the route chosen intersection by intersection. Intersections were few, yet they still outnumbered vehicles. I should warn you that cruel winters and even nastier Harris-cutbacks have resulted in no shortage of frost heaves and potholes on the secondary roads. So forget about riding any racer-poser with punitive riding position and limited suspension travel. As for the main provincial highways, Mikey's generosity toward friends in the construction business has steered tens of millions of tax dollars toward the elimination of all hills and corners in these parts, eliminating much of the reason to visit the area. Perhaps there was a shortage of friends in the water-purification business. Anyway, whatever you decide to bring along for the ride, expect bumps. Bumps mean less traffic, more curves, and better scenery. I only mention this because as we've yet to ride together, I don't know how you feel about such roads.

We'll risk it
This Sunday we found some pretty dreadful pavement. Fortunately, the first batch ended at the ROAD NOT MAINTAINED, USE AT OWN RISK sign. This proved a great trail—narrow, the bush brushing handlebar ends around blind corners. There was one particularly neat section where the path nervously stretched across a swamp, its surface an inch at best above black water lapping to either side. It wouldn't take much of a wave to flood the road.

Recent heavy rains made a mess of the steep bits, but it was nothing a good rider on a Gold Wing couldn't handle. And it was beautiful, the sun slicing shards of light across the road as autumn teased the trees with a blush of colour.

Back on pavement, we ran through marginal farmland, fields unfenced, grasses creeping up through pavement's edge. A few small square-cut log houses leaned in toward the road among even fewer modern intrusions, such as the '70s-trendy geodesic dome. Pavement switched to roly-poly gravel (dreadful crap to travel over, even on four wheels), then hard-pack gravel, then back to pavement as we passed Eau Claire Gorge. Used to be a nifty place to hike around back in the days when my back used to like to hike around nifty places. Ratty pavement continued to carry us through a fun collection of curves and valleys along a road I had somehow overlooked until this Sunday, ditto the gravel road that followed. That one delivered us to, and through, the back door of 417 Auto Wreckers, past a clutter of abandoned industrial machinery and out onto Hwy 17. I had always thought this road in from the highway was the wrecking yard's driveway, which just goes to prove you should never take any road for granted. We Trans-Canada'ed the short distance to the chip stand.

Lard it on
You ever had poutine? I mean, proper poutine? The kind with heaps of great greasy fries smothered in shredded curds and hot, canned gravy? Sits in the stomach like a fifty-pound bag of cement. Wash it down with a can of Pepsi. Once a year, you need to do this. Jackie and I split a small poutine and one can of Pepsi.

The road north of Mattawa, Hwy 533, begins smooth, running near the Mattawa River, the smooth ending at the road to the ski hill. From there on it's a scrappy bit of trickery, the pavement narrow, poked with rocks, patched and prodded, the surface made permanent washboard by heavy trucks taking the shortcut to and from Quebec. On the right bike it can be a hoot, diving into tight 90s, the wheels hopping about, cutting makeshift apexes between hobbled pavement and dirt. Really helps to settle the poutine. True, there's the occasional hunter's pickup rounding a corner on your side pulling a trailer-load of ATVs, but hey, hunters from the south bring dollars to the north. And bullets. The bumps end at Hwy 63, a could-be-fast-if-it-weren't-so-fanatically-patrolled highway that smooths its way back homeward.

Anyway, what I'm getting at is next time we'll ignore the weather forecast. At least it's you who will be riding home in the cold and rain. Although it could be snow by then if you listen to those weather bamboozlers. Unless it surprises everybody with warm sunshine.

Your fellow CC contributor, Max.

Put the best to rest

January 2001

Lately I've been buried in a barrage of alleged best roads. You know, "the best road in (your province here)," that sort of thing. Being a keen fan of great roads, my interest ignites every time I'm confronted with such a claim. Yet typically, once I discover what road is being nominated, my response is "Yeah, that's a good road, but I know of an even better one."

All of which set my mind's wheels spinning—how could there be so many "best"? And what constitutes "best"? That's how I came to realize "the best road" doesn't exist. I know this is a bit like telling the kiddies Santa's a scam, but it's not my fault—reality is a mean-spirited despot.

How many times have you ridden a road, stopped at its end,

Some words should be restricted, requiring prior approval (from me, naturally) before use. "Best" is one of them, for in reality it rarely exists. But then, what do I know about reality?
—Max

maybe removed your helmet in wonder, and exclaimed "Golly, that's gotta be the best road in the whole wide world, better even than (insert name of famed road here)" or some such drivel? Certainly I'm guilty on a few counts. Even put my foolishness into print. Once, when I first started writing for this rag, I claimed there was no need to go to California with roads such as those in Ontario's Haliburton area to ride, an interesting assertion considering I had yet to visit California. Having since been to California a few times, I still think there's no real need to visit there, but in general it does have better motorcycling roads than Ontario. But not the best roads.

Road rashness
When appraising a road's worth, impressions are invariably influenced by all manner of extraneous stuff. A miserable rain driven sideways by a bitchin' cold north wind under a forever blackened sky is bound to taint a rider's judgment of, and enthusiasm for, the value of a chosen route, as will the reverse—sunshine, warm days, and blue skies. So weather is an important element in anointing "best" status. Then there's the vehicle.

Although I've no proof to back me up on this, I suspect that few roads have been named "best" from an aisle seat, halfway back, of an inter-city bus. Yet on the ideal motorcycle, in perfect weather, even parts of the Trans-Canada Highway can seem a great place to travel. For some folks almost any activity can be improved with the addition of a good friend, while others prefer to go it alone. Either way, travelling companions will alter perceptions of a road. And what about traffic? From my perspective, it's tough to top the pleasure of an empty road. And what about perspective? Mine states that best roads aren't the fastest ways to get anywhere, though often they are the roads I travel the fastest. Another personal component is mood. Some days the world is just Jim-dandy, while at other times it sucks big time, though a good road always seems to improve things for me (perhaps making a road seem even better than if I had been in a good mood to start?).

Because roads travel through the world, how humanity and nature present themselves—assuming you're travelling slow enough to notice—can turn a mediocre bit of roadery into a grand excursion. Also, new experiences typically seem more dramatic than tried-and-true greatness. And don't discount food. A piece of pie, pastry perfectly flaked and stuffed with fresh fruit, can increase the worth of a road faster than it can increase a waistline. Reality warps to fit the occasion.

Today's nirvana is...
Yet certainly the most important ingredient in any road review is that which precedes it. Find two connected curves in southern Manitoba—with a hill—and someone will allege to have stumbled upon sport-bike nirvana simply because everything adjacent to it—in every direction—is so damned straight and flat. Conversely, it's easy to get complacent about yet another batch of scenic twisties in B.C. after you've spent the past three days riding through scenic twisties in B.C. None of B.C.'s wealth detracts from that bit of nirvana in topographically impoverished Manitoba, but if you had just been air-lifted from B.C. to this prairie candidate for bestest, you would question what the fuss was about. Great roads need to be ridden to, not just ridden on. And maybe you don't like curves, in which case you're reading the wrong magazine.

But what really tosses "best" labels into the roadside trash can is that to choose "best," you—personally—need to have sampled them all. In the same conditions, frame of mind, etc. And who's travelled all the roads? Hell, I haven't even hit every road in my own neighbourhood. Not that I haven't tried. Spread out a map, of any region, and there—more of the little twisted buggers staring at me, untravelled, taunting me to come ride them. And I need to do this; it's an addiction.

Anyway, no more "best" for me. "One of the best," sure, or better still, "one of my favourites." That works; covers all the variables. Sure, I bought the myth in the past, even anointed a few "best road" candidates, but no more. Reality has resurfaced my perspective—the best road doesn't exist. Of course, none of this will stop me from looking, especially since Santa just brought me some new maps for Christmas.

Reason and prudence

February 2001

Once upon a time, speed on Montana's highways was regulated by the phrase "reasonable and prudent." This enlightened approach to traffic management died when the U.S. government instigated a national speed limit of 55 mph. Then in December, 1995, Washington backed off and Montana reverted to the "reasonable and prudent" rule. At least until 1999. Faced with several appeals on convictions for speeding, the Montana Supreme Court decided that a police officer cannot cite someone for speeding when that person doesn't "reasonably know what speed will violate the law," it being at the sole discretion of the officer, not the operator of the vehicle, to decide what constitutes reasonable and prudent. So with that rule canned, for a short while

Right from birth, humanity is led around on a leash, generally acquiring a preference for a leash-controlled life. So could it be—as some folks have suggested—that I'm not human? Perhaps, but it never ceases to amaze me how much freedom humans are prepared to relinquish in exchange for some other person or institution taking over the responsibilities of decision-making. Is it the fear of being wrong, or even right, that's behind this phenomenon? Or perhaps it's simply the fear of being different? I'll ask the wife if I can answer that.
—Max

AROUND THE BEND (AGAIN)

Montana had no highway speed limits. This fun quickly ended when the state opted for numerical limits, such as its 70-mph daytime limit for two-lane highways. Although a damn sight better than similar Canadian limits, it's the abolition of "reasonable and prudent"–not the limits to speed itself–that troubles me.

Who better to establish what is "reasonable and prudent" than the operator of the vehicle? Road conditions, weather, traffic, and the operator's ability and comfort level dealing with these variables all change. No one is in a better position to assess these changes than the vehicle's operator. That the operator is in most cases incapable of making that assessment is not a fault of the "reasonable and prudent" rule, but of the government's unwillingness to insist the operator have the skills required to make that assessment. Truth is, most people are incapable of safely operating their vehicle of choice at the restrictive limits placed on Canadian highways, let alone Montana's current higher limits. And don't even think about letting them decide for themselves.

Kid's skid school
When raising my son, I tried to avoid enforcing the usual raft of parental "safety" restrictions. I knew he would likely disobey most of them anyway (hard to believe now, but I was once young myself). Instead, I endeavoured to give him the skills to do things, even the risky stuff. So rather than refusing to let him cross the road, I taught him how to cross the road. Obviously, I couldn't always be there to watch over him and see that he did it correctly, but at least he had the skills. Had I taken the easy route and made crossing the road illegal, he would have still crossed, if only to get to the other side, while lacking the knowledge of how to safely accomplish the task.

Much later, when he came of driver's licence age, he took the usual driver's ed course to make him eligible for insurance discounts. But before allowing him to proceed to the government's parallel-park-a-car-and-pass test, he had to know more. Fortunately, his previous years of dirt biking experience made my job substantially easier. Still, when winter hit, we went out on the ice and did endless doughnuts until he knew how to control a slide. We even wore out a set of tires practising emergency stops in a deserted paved parking lot. And I taught him how to drive fast, for it's criminally naive of parents to assume that their children will never exceed posted limits. Basically, I made sure he had the skills to assess the variables and set his pace accordingly. In other words, to operate his vehicle of choice in a reasonable and prudent manner. This might on occasion contravene the laws of the land; far more important is his safety and the safety of others who may be sharing the road.

Speaking of others, what's the point of acquiring advanced skills when some bozo with thoughts stuck in a cellphone can come careening over the crest of a hill in an air-bagged SUV, dead-centre, and take you out on your motorcycle? Because those skills will allow you to not only avoid your own stupidity but also the stupidity of others.

Fast cash flow
Regrettably, North American governments universally set abysmally low standards for vehicle operator licenses. This justifies the maintenance of artificially low speed limits in order to minimize the damage when we inevitably bump into each other. "Speed kills" only because road users lack the skills necessary to safely use the road. And governments have reasons to keep things as they are. For one thing, the enforcement of speed laws is revenue positive. Enforcing real crimes—such as murder or rape—costs the government money. Without the added cash flow generated by ticketing, how can bloated government salaries and expense accounts be paid (particularly in this age of tax-cut mania)? Speed limits also give governments control, and governments would rather you be out of control on the road than to be out of their control. And in the end, control is what it's really about. To teach those in your charge, and to allow them to make decisions based on that knowledge, is to lose control. So parents avoid it, bosses avoid it, religions avoid it, and governments most definitely avoid it. Is it any wonder then that the imposition and enforcement of speed limits has become such a societal priority?

Been there, bought the T-shirt

March 2001

We met at a truck-stop in Newfoundland. It had been raining hard all day, was still raining as we sat across from each other, rainsuits dripping puddles onto linoleum, wet gloves steaming on the baseboard heater beside us. He was riding a Gold Wing. He was American. So naturally it wasn't long into our mediocre meal of mush that he began reciting his "been there, seen that, bought the T-shirt" litany of motorcycle exploits. There were no descriptives, simply the listing of dates and place names. All memorized. Ten minutes of this and I thought, geez, this guy's got no place left to go. Anyway, with the arrival of apple pie and ice cream, he corked his monologue and we consumed a surprisingly good dessert in silence. Then, as

Another look the art of travel without seeing anything, a return to the theme of Around the Bend, August, 1985, sort of. Despite assertions to the contrary, we are all susceptible to the lure of judging the success of a voyage by the distance travelled rather than the enjoyment of the adventure, probably because humanity must quantify everything in order to evaluate its worth. (I give the above comments four out of five stars.)
—Max

the last crumbs of pie crust were forked off his plate, he asked where I was headed.

"Red Bay, Labrador," I replied.

An eyebrow raised. He hadn't been there. In affected casualness painfully devoid of subtlety, he pried for information—where was Red Bay, how do you get there? He and I both knew what a fine feather this would be in his travel cap. So I laid it on thick, blah, blah, tourist-brochure blah. We parted with the usual "perhaps we'll see you again" stuff and rode off separately into the rain.

Tour doer
Two days later in Labrador, as I was about to bed down at Barney's Hospitality Home in L'Anse-au-Loop, my truck-stop companion reappeared. Along with the rain. The last ferry of the day had just deposited him. He was going to ride to Red Bay the next morning, then catch the first ferry back to Newfoundland. Fortunately, I had already been to Red Bay in the dry and actually bought a T-shirt, a welcome addition to any wardrobe after three weeks on the road without laundromats.

About five the next morning I awoke to pitch black and the muffled sound of a Gold Wing in the pounding rain. Prying back a peek-a-boo sliver of curtain, a flashing blur of red signalled a right turn out of Barney's driveway. The Gold Wing was headed for Red Bay. This is really stupid, I thought. It's cold out there, monsoon-wet, a thick stew of blackness and fog obscuring vision, and this guy is going to ride the only twisted road in Labrador, a narrow trace of pavement that squiggles through a wonderfully scenic valley of steep drop-offs, and ride back again to the ferry just to add Red Bay to his list of been-theres. There was no chance of seeing a damn thing except the centreline of the road. If he was lucky. He might as well have stayed in bed and lied about the trip for all that he'd see.

There are more reasons to ride a motorcycle than there are motorcycles, each reason legitimate to its inventor, yet I have some difficulty understanding the faction that collects destinations as the children of England used to collect vehicle licence numbers (and perhaps still do—the Brits are an odd bunch). It's a collection mania, one that exists simply to add another entry to a list in order to boast to others with lists of similar non-purpose, for who else would care? This group has close links to the kilometre catchers who take great pride in ultra-high odometer readings. BMW owners seem to be particularly odometrically anal, Beemer clubs proudly listing members reportedly reaching some predetermined level of greatness, measured in distance (another so-what list). But what have any of you seen? I mean, beyond the roll-over of numbers and WELCOME TO ANYTOWN, PLEASE DRIVE CAREFULLY signs? Bugger all, I suspect.

Pride goeth, and goeth...
So it was with some surprise that I found myself caught up in this same enterprise, choosing to embark on a one-day ride to some faraway, god-forgotten hole noir in northern Quebec on a day the cold air was soaked in a fog so thick I could almost read the road using Braille as effectively as by sight. I endured this grief until the fog collapsed under its own weight, ripping away from the grey cloud above, leaving only me and the cold to share the road below with a smattering of travellers in enclosed, heated vehicles. I seldom stopped, riding fast, driven by destination, got there, wondered why, and turned tail for home. Fortunately, the fog packed it in for my return trip, though the world remained decidedly dreary as I droned through grey skies, grey pavement, grey denuded trees. It was more like some hemorrhoidal Hoogeveen endurance test than a tour. Yet—as I began to realize to my dismay—there's a peculiar satisfaction to enduring, an unjustifiable feeling of accomplishment, even when that accomplishment is pointless. Every kilometre passed becomes another notch in the barrel of the goal—or is the accumulation of notches the real goal?

I have no answer for that. Maybe the next time my pal Peter Hoogeveen runs the Blackfly endurance ride out of North Bay I'll ask him or a few of the participants—why stay up 24 hours to ride in unpleasant conditions at high speed simply to get back to where you just left? Or maybe I won't, for do I really need an answer other than there sure are a lot reasons to ride a motorcycle?

Make plans to improvise

May 2001

It was just a squiggly black line, one of many running ragged and unnumbered across the Washington state map. This one not only had the distinction of passing right below Mount St. Helens, it was also part of our chosen route to Seattle. The weather waffled between late winter and early spring, nursing a bad attitude. The ranger in front of us wasn't so ambivalent. The forest roads to the north were definitely closed in all directions, washed out by recent heavy rainfalls. Scratch one carefully planned itinerary.

Under a sky blanked out by light grey, the air whispered of rain, oozing a cool mist that clung to everything from spiders' webs to helmet visors. All dressed up in rainsuits with no apparent place to go, Jackie suggested we ride

Despite my occasional attempts to plan—tours, house-building, things that need to be done during my next trip into town, whatever—life for me is primarily an improvised existence. So far, this is good.
—Max

to the CLOSED sign. The ranger openly questioned her wisdom but I brushed aside his cautions. No point in explaining—he obviously didn't understand the power of a whim. Hell, Jackie and I got married on one.

The road to CLOSED cavorted along the Wind River in solitude, temperature quickly losing degrees to altitude. A modest sign to the Government Mineral Springs beckoned and we swapped asphalt for gravel, taking a deep breath to squeeze between towering cedars boasting trunks wider than our saddlebagged bike. A makeshift macadam of sticks and stones ended at a turn-around, the foliage above letting only sliver-thin shafts of light poke through. At the spring's wellhead, a traditional hand-pump spit out horrible-tasting water. Eighty years ago, rich folks travelled for thousands of miles to sample this stuff. Now, they drink Perrier in the comfort of their own homes.

Tippler's travel

Back on the main route, we followed its tortuous path northward along the river as curve after curve tossed switchbacks up into the mountains, swooping this way and that, steep drop-offs unguarded by rail or fence. We rode through drizzle, the road lined in snow, to the ROAD CLOSED sign, turned around and reversed our track. The depth of each drop-off was more evident now, staring us in the face as we descended past the spring, easing out of the clouds to eventually meet a numbered highway that entwined with a railway along the north shore of the Columbia River.

On to plan B, as yet to be defined. Heading east, another black map-squiggle willed us to the village of Corner where an eatery invited us in. I sauntered to the bar and asked a patron about the road north.

"Don't take it." The advice arrived on a waft of alcohol fumes. Our travel consultant—a rugged-faced man of undetermined age but certainly old enough to accumulate some unhealthy history—had difficulty issuing his words as separate units. "Ev'rybody goesup tha' damroad. Boring's hell. You wanna nice road, take the Glenwood Valley road—nobody onit, pretty as all get out—there," he pointed out the window as he paused for a sip of liquid refreshment. So on a fume-driven whim, we aimed east to go north.

Survey me not

A modest line of pavement led us into cattle country. To my reckoning, the road must have faithfully followed the original wagon trail, as it contained a wonderful bundle of curves and small rises that no modern surveyor would have left unbulldozed. Trees crowded around creek and river beds as sun-bleached, pale-green fields sprawled across the remainder of the valley floor. In the distance, a warm sun lit the snow-cap of Mount Adams, all roads around it closed, apparently.

Farther east, open range eased up into the trees as flashes of a mighty canyon flickered through the conifers—a wall of vertical, grey rock occasionally glimpsed from a speeding motorcycle. The road began to toss and turn, curling and coiling around on itself as it plummeted into Willis Canyon, almost kissed the Klickitat River on a small bridge, twirled around and flung itself up the other side where previously steep, solid rock became piles of loose stone and red rubble. We hunted the fast line along this stretch of roadway, a sinuous striped snake that darted in and out of sight, slithering along the edge of the canyon, gouging a narrow shelf into a canyon wall that sloped at about 45 degrees, its rock and rubble held in place by a few token shrubs, fewer scrawny trees, a rag-tag collection of wild grasses, and not much else—a reassuring thought.

As road spun out of canyon, it found flatter land and fewer trees. Yet, even when uncalled for, it still danced a curve, the straight stretches connected by frequent 90-degree turns for no apparent reason. Could the road's designer have been a motorcyclist? Goldendale is where whim met the reality of major highway, and we headed north until we met trucks decorated in snow following their descent from the mountain pass. A vacancy sign and promises of GOOD FOOD beckoned, and we answered. That evening, good intentions suggested we plan for the next day, but instead we switched out the lights, crawled into bed, and listened to the rain pounding on the cabin's roof. Some things you just can't seem to plan for.

Running on emptiness

June 2001

It's flat, oh so terribly flat, a pacific piece of the the planet so untroubled by geographic disturbance I can clearly see where land and sky meet about 25 kilometres ahead of me. No matter how fast or slow I ride, this mystical point of rendezvous remains in the distance, taunting me. Catch me if you can, it calls. Okay, okay, the land's not one hundred per cent flat, otherwise there wouldn't be a horizon. And if it weren't for that curvature of the earth, there wouldn't be a bend in sight, so I guess I've got the horizon to thank for that. But from where I'm sitting, the thing that troubles more is the train. It too boasts no end in sight, a length of freight filing out onto the prairies as if in continual assembly just beyond the horizon, that bit of

As mentioned before, I really do enjoy trying to place the reader there, along with me, seeing what I see, feeling what I feel. If you take the time to look, and feel, rare is the spot on this planet not worthy of such attention. And for me, this is especially true for those places that the rest of humanity has bypassed for busier pastures.
—Max

world I can never reach. So I could be here for weeks watching spray-bomb graffiti roll by, clickety-clack, clickety-clack.

Curves, you say?
The day started at Wildwood Sports in Winnipeg. I was getting a new rear tire installed, premature tire wear unfortunately being proportional to a tire's exposure to immature riding techniques. Yet more important than new tread, I needed a good alternative to the north-south boredom of Hwy 75. This is the stretched line of busy pavement that connects the Canada-U.S. border to Winnipeg much as a string connects a child's hand to a helium-filled balloon. (At least a balloon gets set free now and then.)

Try St. Mary's Road south out of town, I was advised, it has curves. Any suggestion that a road in southern Manitoba might deviate from straight is worth pursuing, so that's where I took the new treads. And darned if there aren't curves. Gentle ones, mind you, the road meandering with the Red River as the shade of tall trees occasionally visits the pavement in a most unprairie-like manner. There are no hills to brag about, but it's a pleasant ride.

Too soon, the road–now Hwy 200–leaves the river to parley with a few bilingual communities. Gone are the curves. And the trees now gather in small islands of distant green, floating in an endless sea of yellowed grains. Then suddenly, more green, an isolated field standing so tall it hides the horizon. Industrial hemp. It looks just like marijuana, but the only way it will get anyone high is to make a rope and hang them from one of the grain elevators poking into the blue but otherwise featureless sky. In partnership with the land, this road–like every road around here–is oh so very flat. And straight. And empty. There's not even a gull or a crow staked out on the long-distance power lines that embroider the fields' edges. Which makes having to stop for this train all the more peculiar. Nothing for kilometres this way or that except for this damn train. I could see it coming, even tried to beat it to the crossing, but that proved as fruitful as chasing horizons. So the bike is parked at the crossing, ignition off, the bike's yellow paint fanned by the flashing red lights of the crossing. I'm next to the bike, sitting in the yellowed grass at pavement's edge trying to figure out why I'm having such a good time.

Straight shot
It's the emptiness. For me, the value of space, of an uninhabited road,

has never been questioned. But it's here, seated on prairie turf with a straw dangling thoughts from pensive lips, that the full worth of this vacuous expanse registers. It is sacred, even more so than a twisted bit of pavement. I love a twisty road and will—no coaxing needed—ride umpteen kilowhatevers out of my way merely to chase a rumour of a curve. Yet pack some twisted, frolicking prince of pavement with a rudely disorganized horde of humanity and it just can't compare to the enjoyment of riding this vacated, long and decidedly straight highway. Clickety-clack, the train rattles by, its singular intrusion emphasizing the absence of humanity rather than taking away from it, for there are no other vehicles waiting on my side of the tracks.

The train owns no caboose to punctuate its end nor does it need one as an ever-widening gap between horizon and freight cars approaches. I get back on the bike, ready to ride, not wanting to look like a complete dolt to the occupants of the inevitable pickup trucks parked on the other side of the tracks. But as the train kisses the crossing goodbye, there are no vehicles. Not even a combine. I'm alone. In a reflective mood, I'm struck by Zen-like insights, such as, if a train-crossing signal flashes and clangs, and no one is there to see or hear it, who cares?

That's the other thing about empty highways—with no vehicular silliness to contend with except of one's own making, the lack of traffic and other distractions reward a traveller with ample opportunity to consider some really dumb ideas. Voltaire along dotted line. But mostly, it's the unoccupied space that delights, the inexplicable satisfaction of being the sole person to witness the day from here, wherever here may be. And thanks to a bike's raised perch, an empty world looks all the more deserted when on a motorcycle chasing horizons that continually tease the distance. Even when that chase is periodically interrupted by hemp and choo-choo graffiti.

The atlas un-shrugged

August 2001

Get out the travel map of New Brunswick and draw a triangle roughly bounded by Upper Gagetown, Saint John, and Moncton. Now erase Highways 1 and 2. What you are left with is a delightfully latticed collection of seldom-used backroads—600, 700, and 800 series local highways plus many others that don't even appear on the map, each carrying tons more scenery than traffic. Bisecting the triangle, I was riding east on Hwy 124, a road that pleasantly parallels an arm of the Saint John River. Where 124 jogs south at Springfield, I continued easterly, the lonely roads carrying me through a mellow mix of marginal and prosperous farms, bush, and rusted tractors sitting knee-deep in tall grasses. The pavement was pinched between green fields, bobbing about

Exploring life and backroads without the restraints of destinations—it's all part of the same journey. So let the backroads of life take you where they lead and enjoy the caprice of the moment.
—Max

hills and valleys, cedar-shake barns occasionally caught napping next to my right elbow, a small house sometimes crowding the opposite edge.

It's the sort of neighbourhood that doesn't surprise a visitor to discover all the tombstones in a weed-cluttered graveyard marked with the same last name. Downtown Havelock, on the front porch of Charlie's Grocery, size-large locals loudly conversed in an accent surely stolen from the southern U.S., the gossip laced in long vowels as I sipped on an iced-tea and learned of who's marrying who, and who's not, and who's moving, none of this happening to the purveyors of the gossip, especially the bits associated with moving. Unless it was time for another soda. But I'm getting ahead of where I was headed with this, for it was back in Head of Millstream that the idea first took root.

Backroad to Damascus
I had stopped a few metres south of Hwy 880 on an unnamed sideroad, parking in front of a time-greyed, roadside farmhouse draped in vines. It made for a wonderful photo (excuse the modesty) but what stirred my interest more was the road. Mottled pavement seductively curved just where it ducked out of sight into a valley, teasing me to come chase its course. True,

I encounter hundreds of similar temptations, maybe even thousands, on every tour. Even in my own backyard, every year I manage to find some new-to-me road, some temptress bypassed on my last ride-by. So what's the big deal about this one? Nothing. Except this is where the link between knowledge and roads ran over me.

Neither knowledge nor roads own a destination. When knowledge works as it should, the more we learn, the more we realize we don't know, each fact inevitably yielding more questions than answers, each axiom never fully explored. If you think you know the subject, it simply means you've shutdown the learning process, whether the benchmark for your ignorance be junior kindergarten or a PhD. Same goes for roads, a ride through any area revealing don't-know-how-many avenues with no time this time to explore.

That's why I have trouble revisiting the same place, at least by the same route. Instead, I search for new ways to get there, or alternatives to get away from there, wherever there resides on this occasion. Sadly, I will never be satisfied until I've explored all the roads, and even then I will need to go back and check out the ones I sampled first, because for sure something has changed since I was last there.

Never-ending story
Destinations are artificial limits established by humanity. They don't exist naturally. Admittedly, destinations are often a convenient way to tidy things up, whether searching for a cure for post-nasal drip or choosing a place to go riding. Yet I try to keep mine vague, leaving me the luxury to chase another route along the way–or a different destination–should the urge take hold. Heck, even with dead-ends you can turn around and try another approach. Not that this makes for a contented life, but, contrary to popular myth, even cows aren't contented or they wouldn't be continually stretching necks out beyond the fence in search of greener grass. Contentment is reserved for sedentary humans, at least while the batteries in the channel-changer hold out.

Sorry–I lost sight of my destination. Back on the road this column was originally taking me, after my return from the triangle, I discovered a great book, the *New Brunswick Atlas*, jointly published by Nimbus Publishing and Service New Brunswick (ISBN 1-55109-224-7). At about 100 spiral-bound, 13x10 pages, it's too big to take on the bike, but for preliminary research, or simply as a catalyst to exploration, it's a dandy–full colour, with enough roads to keep an inquisitive motorcyclist busy into his or her next life. Look, there's the road heading south out of Head of Millstream. I didn't succumb to temptation when there, but I will on my next ride through the triangle, perhaps riding it south to Hwy 890. Although the atlas reveals a nifty looking east-west route just a tad south of Hwy 890, which connects to Hwy 895, but if approached from the other end, running through Plumseweep, I could hook up with Hwy 111, which is a treat to ride, even if it lies out of the triangle. Hmm. It looks as if my next visit to New Brunswick might be a long one.

Does it hurt to smile?

September/October 2001

Hwy 524 is short blast of equal parts rough and smooth pavement, divided midpoint by Commanda Creek, with more curves than straight bits to entertain you either side of the single-lane bridge. I had just arrived at its southern end, the first rider of the CVMG Nipissing Section's annual Ride Round the Pond. Leading-edge vintage, if I had been riding a vintage bike. I wasn't, but it's no matter in this group—as long as the vehicle's got two wheels and a motor, you're welcome. In fact, you're welcome regardless. The pond in question was Lake Nipissing, the day was sunny, and we certainly weren't the only group out to enjoy the circuit. There were touring clubs collecting bug guts on large windshields, sport riders

Just one small attempt to help remove the elitist broom from the Harley rider's ass. Perhaps they might smile more without the burden of this affliction.
–Max

gathering fewer splats on smaller windshields, all manner of insecticidal motorcyclists, maybe 200 bikes in all, spread out along the route in clumps of combustion, killing bugs.

Put off a happy
Across from me in the parking lot of an overpriced service-station/country-store stood a platoon of parked Harleys, the local HOG chapter neatly lined up, about to rumble away. And there, near the front, was JR. It wasn't his bike I recognized—frankly, those FL-whatevers all look alike to an eye not trained in the bizarre nuances of Harley-Davidson nomenclature. Nor did I notice him because of his garb, despite the fact that it's a heavily-fringed tan instead of ubiquitous black. No, the reason I instantly picked him out from the rest was that he was the only one of the bunch smiling. I rode over, guiding my decidedly filthy dual-sport through glistening chrome, pinstriped panels of many colours, and studded leather to greet JR. We exchanged broad smiles, a few chuckles, and shook hands as the sneers around us intensified.

So what's with those Harley dudes anyway? Standing around, removed from their bikes, most are cordial and quick to smile. But once seated on their moto-pride, a perpetual scowl invades. Jeez, if it's that painful an experience, why bother? Sell the damn bike and take up curling or some other innocuous pastime. But the truth is, it isn't painful. I've ridden a few Harleys over the years and had a hoot on each. You might have even seen me—I was the one without the beard who was smiling. JR's the one who surrounds his smile in facial fur. So that's two people who think riding a Harley can be fun. Besides hair, another characteristic that differentiates JR from me is that while I have only tasted the Harley experience, JR has been riding one since he was about three. The same one by all appearances. And he's still smiling. I'm not talking about some pasted-on idiot grin the likes of which Gold Wing riders might proffer as they parade teddy bears past the judging stand, but instead a subtle reaction that occurs naturally when having a good time. So why do most Harleyists appear to be suffering? Obviously there has to be a reason beyond the bike itself for their apparent discomfort and displeasure. Could it be that HOG actually stands for Hemorrhoid Owners Group? That could explain the pained visage.

Bugged life
Now that I think about it, the Harleys I rode had original-equipment

exhaust systems. So maybe it's the obnoxious racket emanating from straight pipes that brings them such pain, particularly when clamoured together in cacophonous formation. And here's another thought. Most Harleys I rode while wearing a fullface helmet. Blasphemous by cruiser standards, I know, Harleyites and assorted clones generally preferring to don plastic yarmulkes and bits of beat-up Tupperware as riding headgear. And if the law didn't demand that modicum of hat fashion, no doubt most of them would ride helmetless (assuming they already aren't, their pick of hairnet hardly a helmet by any definition). Not that I have a problem with this—their right of choice, I figure. Still, imagine a cutting wind ripping up the nostrils and into the eyes, pasting eyelids to eyebrows. If that doesn't erase a smile, surely the bugs will. By the time I spotted JR, the shield on my helmet had been thoroughly spotted in insectacolour—smudge-black, bilious-green, and snot-yellow the predominant hues. Try smiling with that mess stuck to your mug.

Then again, maybe that perpetual scowl is evidence of some mandatory sufferance, the sort the religiously inclined often feel the need to endure en route to greater rewards. Certainly there are parallels in the degree of blind worship. But what better reward could there be than to participate in the pleasures of a warm, sunny day aboard a motorcycle? So I'm at a loss as to why any of these grumps-apparent look so grouchy. Fun is not supposed to hurt that much. But the phenomenon does offer a possible explanation as to why so few Harleyians wave as I ride by—if you were that pissed-off, would you wave to people enjoying themselves? So here's a tip to grumpy riders of any brand: Try thinking about all the biting bugs you're bumping into every time you ride, each black fly, mosquito, deer fly and horse fly now dead or disabled. If you live in Canada, that's got to make you smile.

On the road again

January 2002

Thirty-one years ago, I drove Justin to the hospital. I didn't know it was Justin at the time, and I doubt he took much notice of my largesse. He was still in his mother's womb, his mother complaining of labour pains, me quite pleased how this situation seemed to grant a legal excuse to speed. Not that an Austin Mini was ever quick to speed, but tiny pedal-to-the-metal, Jackie and I got to the hospital well before Justin did. And in so doing, it's possible we set a precedent.

Since that day, Justin and I have travelled together extensively, sharing a vehicle when he was young—cars, toboggans, boats, motorcycles, whatever—more often than not at speeds faster than your average user. After he got his own dirt bike, and then car, we even travelled

Together, my son, Jeff, and I have ridden dirt bikes, played hockey, gone snowboarding and hiking. But we've never gone for a road ride together. In this column, Max explains the special relationship that lucky fathers have with their sons. It is difficult to put into words how the birth of my first child affected my outlook on life and how it seemed to suddenly put the whole world into perspective. Through Max, I was able to vicariously share my love of my son with the love of motorcycling.
—Bill Coghill

For most people, it's easier to express a love for a close friend in print or in song. As I no longer write songs, I used this column to voice the relationship I have with my son.
—Max

separately together, if you know what I mean. But save for a couple of much-too-brief encounters, the shared experience of riding our own street bikes together passed us by. Life got in the way, schedules didn't mesh, distances apart became greater, and every visit we were either up to our collective armpits in snow or stuff needed to be hauled from here to there (like families, for instance), which usually dictated the dreaded four-wheels, under-one-roof option. Then Justin's wife got her own motorcycle, making it two bikes in his and her garage. And can you believe the coincidence? I just happen to have brought my riding gear along. With the universe thus lined up and in tune with a late-summer sunny afternoon, Justin and I opened the garage door.

What have we here...
Neither bike is fancy-new; his, in fact, is a bike I rebuilt from a wreck about 15 years ago and subsequently sold. The bike has recently, and serendipitously, returned to the family fold like a lost cat. It's spitting out a bit of oil here and there, and over there too, but still doing the job. Judged by current standards of necessity, both bikes come up short, too small to be taken seriously by the colourful-leather crowd. "Good beginner bikes" an ad might read. Perfect bikes, in other words, on which to begin our inaugural joint street ride.

Justin lives in the nation's capital, a city situated a tad north and east of some of Ontario's best motorcycling country. Trouble is, to get to the good stuff we must first endure about an hour's worth of land as flat as Stockwell Day's ideas, through fields as empty as Gilles Duceppe's head, traversed by roads as straight as Joe Clark, battling traffic as thick as the bureaucracy surrounding Jean Chrétien, which normally would be as pointless as Alexa McDonough except that eventually, as the lumps of Parliament Hill fade behind us, I am again reminded what a wonderful place Canada can be.

Traffic thins as this nation's most valuable resource–space–opens up before us. The curves begin fast and sweeping along Tennyson Road, the terrain starting to yield hints of hills. We backroad into Perth, stop for gas, head north, then west, then lost. Okay, so I was leading, but there was this road not on the map that needed to be surveyed, and anyway the main thing is it wasn't long before we ended up on County Road 36 pointed south for Westport. Leading in and out and around Westport–a quaint village of touristy-type buildings–hides a twisted jumble of roads, all dandies, most sinuous streaks of tarmac scampering over countless hills while dodging forested, ragged-rock scenery. County Road 36 is my favourite of the group.

Today's pace–faster than a speeding Mini–is working for both of us, the space between bikes comfortable and constant no matter which one is leading or who is riding which bike. It's as if we have been riding together for years, which of course we have, just–until now–on different roads. Like long-time riding partners, we even debate which Westport ice cream parlour to patronize. The one I favour has parking right out front, so I win. Unfortunately, I think I also bought.

Cycles within cycles
On our way back to the city of capital lies, we find gravel (North Shore Road, a wonderfully twisted bit of dust and marbles) and again, neither rider exercises any advantage. Or much restraint, for that matter. Back on pavement, speeds increase, both bikes soon pegged to the stops as Justin and I are once again hurrying to get somewhere we don't have to get to in a hurry. There's no evidence of father/son competition or rivalry, or deference to age in either direction. We're just a couple of guys out for a good time, riding at the edge simply for the pure fun of it.

With driver's licences safely returned to his Ottawa driveway, we both agree it's a good thing we did this on "beginner bikes." Given the historical precedence, no question we would have been tapped out no matter what we were riding. Once out of jackets, Justin says hi to a neighbour who owns an MGB–a close vehicular relative to the aforementioned Mini. I introduce myself. Surprised, the neighbour says, "I thought you were brothers." Riding partners, actually, re-sharing a mutual love of speed first experienced thirty-one years ago.

Note: The names mentioned in describing the land around Ottawa were all leaders of Canadian federal political parties at the time, only two of which still hold that position as I write this, one of those two having announced his upcoming retirement. Naturally, I take full credit for this good news.
–Max

Go fast, save the Earth

February 2002

There's a ton of good reasons to rid the nation's highways of speed limits but perhaps none so compelling as the environmental issue. The enforcement of these antiquated and arbitrary limits, while admittedly good for police and provincial coffers, is wreaking a profound, deleterious effect on the environment. How? Check out the copious pollution spewed by the titanic vehicles of police preference—Chevy Suburbans, Ford Crown Victorias, Chevrolet Impalas, and what's this? Full-size pickup trucks. Bunches of them all decked out in OPP regalia. Like, what the hell? Looks as if any gas-pig is a candidate for cop-cart duty. Count 'em, in every province and territory. Your tax dollars are feeding a huge fleet of gas guzzlers racking up huge distances, most of

Here, I offer an absurd solution to an absurd abuse of privilege. As the described abuse concerns the police, it should come as no surprise that my solution remains the lesser absurdity of the two.
—Max

the racking done well above the posted limits the vehicle operators are sworn to enforce. You would be hard pressed to find a greater single source of air pollution in Canada.

Downsize 'em

Humanity once convinced itself that the world was flat. Obviously, time and discovery has shown this to be false—it's only the eastern prairies that are flat. And maybe the bits around Ottawa and Windsor. Oh yeah, parts of southern Quebec *aussi*. And certainly most of P.E.I. Anyway, it's the same thickheaded approach that clings to the concept of "speed kills," a century-old absurdity emanating from the fear of motorcars first experienced by fans of the horse. Fine, but if society is to continue to believe that fast-travelling vehicles constitute a danger on the highways then we must look at ways to minimize the environmental impact of enforcement.

Top of the list, get rid of that foul fleet of vehicles, exchanging the prodigious polluters for something less environmentally repugnant. How about motorcycles? While it's true that motorcycles in general are less environmentally disruptive, realistically this won't work—our harsh winter climate rules it out. Also, motorcycles lack the room to taxi trouble-makers to jail. And, having witnessed police driving, do we really want to encourage them to ride? Whoa, talk about a danger on the highways. Instead, let's swap Suburbans for four-door diesel VWs (the back seat of the Golf will easily accommodate a couple of size-large criminals—organized or otherwise—or even fold down to transport bulk pepper spray), Crown Vics for Suzuki Sprints (the girls on the force will love these easy-to-park cuties). Instantly, we take millions of litres of hazardous gases and particulates out of the atmosphere.

According to health-department studies, air pollution is killing thousands of Canadians every year, admittedly a debatable guestimate, but undoubtedly many more than any similar death-count attributable to the act of speeding. No question, lives would be saved merely by switching to fuel-miserly vehicles. Then subtract the added pollution cost of manufacturing your typical bozomobile—the extra metal, reams of recalled-rubber, pounds of plastic, and smelly sweat—and the air is starting to smell sweeter already.

Even if you don't give a rat's ass about the environment, consider the huge sums of money provincial governments could save from the change-over, both in operating costs and capital expenditures. And think of the savings in health care costs. Better yet, think of the resultant tax cuts!

Tickety-boo

But let's not stop the environmental wagon there. Do you know how many trees have to be cut down to manufacture a single book of traffic-violation tickets? Neither do I, but likely it's enough to clear-cut a typical much-loved city park. According to the David Suzuki Foundation, over half of all the trees ever cut have been downed since 1967. Clearly it's not just coincidence that during the same period more speeding tickets have been issued than in all preceding time. As forests disappear, the earth's ability to absorb carbon dioxide is proportionately diminished, which in turn causes more greenhouse gases to float up into the atmosphere and eat away at the ozone layer. This equates to increased global warming—the acknowledged cause of freak storms and drought—and dangerously elevated levels of UV rays—the primary cause of skin cancer. Think about it—people are dying all over the world because some cop in Canada just wrote a speeding ticket.

If Canada's para-military must persist in this inhumane activity, then, for the sake of our children, replace tickets with verbal warnings. Warnings are friendly, both from environmental and human perspectives. What's wrong with a nice chat? Internet chat groups are rife with romance—think of the possibilities. Police armour replaced by roadside amour, buttoned uniforms strained by a heavy heave of the heart. Instead of the solemn sound of a judge's gavel denting a bench-top and the public's wallet, maybe we would hear... wedding bells.

Okay, okay, back to plan A. Scrap the speed limit on highways entirely, sell the platoons of excess vehicles, lay off the lunchroom loads of excess staff, and then take a deep breath. It could be the best thing we could ever do for the environment. Mine anyway.

It's just a bike

March 2002

I had known her for years, a business aquaintance, the casual nature of our friendship perpetually maintained by the counter between us. She asked me what kind of motorcycle I had these days, and when I told her, she replied "That must be your baby." It was a sincere comment, one meant to signify understanding. I said "No, it's just a motorcycle." My dismissive response caught her off-guard, and in an odd way, me too. This opinion had not been voiced; it was not an acknowledged part of my philosophy. Until that moment. Motorcycles don't get me horny anymore.

There was a time not that long ago when every year I would salivate over the new models, looking for that one special motorcycle I knew would bring me ultimate

It's amusing that despite the near universal condemnation by the world's religions of humanity's worship of material things, we still love 'em. Advertising has become the new bible, the product the new god. To own is to practice your religion. Owning makes you a better person. But which is the real owner, you or the object of your materialism?

—Max

joy and everlasting contentment. I would make the annual pilgrimage to the bike show, elbow my way past the poseurs (whadda they know—I read the previews in all the mags), and sit on every motorcycle that even remotely seemed seductive. Sometimes I found the ideal bike, sometimes I found several, and every couple of years or so I would buy the hot bike (or bikes) that caused my drool to sizzle. And there's the trouble with contentment—it lacks longevity.

Not that I noticed this truism as it succumbed to my lust. I was an active participant in sustaining the myth of sustainable growth. And in unnerving synchronism, the economy was on a roll when I was buying. But the world's financial health wasn't what motivated me to spend. I was driven by loftier reasons. I would be a better man on a better bike. So what if I had erred with my previous purchase, this latest love was special, definitely the one I had really wanted all along but only now possessed the acumen to recognize. And to be honest, searching for and then buying a new bike was really exciting. It was akin to courtship, only if things didn't work out, it was easier to terminate the relationship.

Baby, it's you
And, again as with courtship, I knew things would work out this time. In common with the bikes of purchases past, this year's best bike would get washed and waxed and polished, but only after all the body parts were stripped off so I could get at those tenacious little bits of unseen grime with toothbrushes and Q-Tips. Everything had to gleam. And it did. After all, it was my baby. Yes, I would ride it too, but every time it rained, or the air gagged with bugs, another day would be spent destroying the evidence of use. Yes indeedy, no finer example of that bike could exist, anywhere. Of course, I wasn't nearly so passionate—or anal—with my dirt bikes. I mean, how could you steer anything you loved into the rocks and mud and brush to be scratched and gouged and dented. Give it a quick hosing down, oil the chain, clean the air filter if I remembered, then park it until the next ride. Dirt bikes got abused; street bikes got pampered. Then I got a dual-purpose bike. Talk about messing with your head space.

Hey, I tried to keep the darn thing clean. After all, it had a street plate on it. But it kept heading for the mud, the dust and the grime.

Then I noticed that on the ride home, if I rode fast enough on the pavement, it was sort-of self-cleaning, the bigger chunks flinging off in manure-spreader fashion. This worked even better after watering-out in rivers that proved surprisingly deeper than surface indications implied, or when I had to lay her down midstream to avoid hitting some endangered fish. Perhaps it was during one such sacrifice for nature that I began to question the merits of the habitual wash-cycle routine, I'm not sure. Re-focused, my new goal was to keep my bikes—street or dirt or both—well-oiled and sort-of clean, and always ready to ride. And slowly, so slow as to be unnoticed by me or my friends, I lost my passion for motorcycles. I didn't love, worship and wash my latest bike—I rode it. My passion for motorcycles had been replaced with a passion for motorcycling.

It's the motion
Not that I wasn't keen on motorcycling before; it's just that the specific bike always held a major portfolio in my moto-psyche. Now, give me anything my worn-out body is up to riding and I'm there, let's ride, who cares what it looks like or whether it's marketed toward sport, touring, cruising, dirt, he-men or pantywaists, as long as it has got two wheels and a motor. The bike goes where I want it to go. And probably won't get washed when I get home. I still appreciate looking at sparkling clean bikes—old, new, whatever—as long as someone else is applying the spit and polish. But I no longer covet them. And that's the other thing. Now when I go to a motorcycle show, I find myself floor-testing few bikes, and those few mostly out of curiosity or simply as a convenient place to sit and rest my abused back. Yet I remain at the show even longer than I used to, not to check out the bikes, but to talk to other motorcyclists, not caring whether they're into shine or into riding. I guess the main thing years of living with a passion has taught me is that a motorcycle without a rider is like a kiss without a partner.

Let me make two points

April 2002

Normally I'm not the sort of gentleman who deals in controversy. Admittedly, this could be because I'm not much of a gentleman, but until the February oh-too issue of *Cycle Canada* I had tactfully avoided being drawn into the debate over Thane Silliker's hasty coast-to-coast rides—no time to stop and pee let alone taste the pie. But in the Readers Write section, Thane himself chose to drag me into the defence of his silliness. So, drawn and dragged, here's my take.

Thane's venture in bladder control is at best an act of vain stupidity and high risk that adds yet another notch on the increasingly crowded barrel of humanity's dumb-gun. But (and that's a bigger but than most armchair critics sit on) my view, and yours too, is largely

> Another case of being drawn into battle by the remarks on that volatile page set aside for a magazine's readers' comments. This time it involves the debate over Mr. Silliker's attempts to set the shortest-time record for crossing Canada on a motorcycle. Perhaps my response is summed up best by the old blues phrase "Ain't nobody's business but my own." Ride what you want, how you want.
> —Max

irrelevant in this case. Thane didn't ask any of us along for the ride, or seek out our permission, or do it to "raise money for charity" (after expenses of course). He just did it, his time, his money, I suspect because—no matter how frivolous or self-serving it might seem on the surface—it was important to him. People risk life and limb to add first accents of mountains to that beguiling barrel on the dumb-gun, sail solo around the world through some of the nastiest conditions on the planet just to be the first to arrive back where they started, telemark over fields of shifting ice through blizzards of sub-frigid weather just to reach some desolate, white flat of real estate surrounded by hundreds of kilometres of more of the same—gawd, is there no limit to what the world's wackos will do to prove a pointless point? Obviously, no. And this is a good thing.

Risky business
Give me your justification for riding a motorcycle. No matter how you cut it, travel by car makes more sense. Of course, cars are also less fun, a trait shared with most things society blesses as sensible and safe alternatives. Motorcyclists know this. Most of us accept the risks inherent with motorcycling in exchange for its greater rewards. So you would think we would understand that the need for risk and adventure can be as intense in some folks as the need for food. Consider this. A blind man climbs Mount Everest and the vast majority of the outdoor community praise his accomplishment, and even put him on the cover of *Outside* magazine. This is a guy who—in common with other daft climbers—risks freak storms, huge falls from ice shields, hypothermia, frostbite, permanent brain damage (if he didn't have it already) from lack of oxygen, just to peak a mountain. And—here's the seriously dumb part—he can't even enjoy the view. Back in the motorcycle camp, Thane crosses Canada in less than 60 hours—a stunt that rivals cresting Mount Everest with your eyes shut for stupidity—and we dump on him. "Yeah, but what about the image of motorcycling?" the clich inevitably calls out. Who cares? That image only sucks if you count yourself among the sensible of society. And besides, what's the point of trying to prove the obvious to the ignorant?

Let's get linear
Some might argue, with some veracity, that life itself is a pointless endeavour. But not me. Make a linear calendar, your birthday at one end, toss a dart and where it lands becomes your death at

the other end. Those are life's two points. Now what are you going to do between those points? You could stay home and watch televised escapades of others celebrating this thing called life. Millions do. Certainly it avoids the aggravation and expense of actually doing something. But how many bank managers, legislators, and insurance agents does this world really need? And why are the world's non-participants typically the first to offer cautions and what-ifs at the mere suggestion of risk? The same ones never to have put a notch on the barrel of the dumb-gun. Or to make a linear calendar.

If there is any act of wrongdoing here it is not Thane's fondness for sleep-deprivation, or a blind man's wish to climb mountains, but society's attempts to rob an individual's right to risk, all in the name of some misconceived general good. Governments would much prefer we all stayed home and behaved ourselves—please use public transit when going out, but do try to get enough exercise so as not to pose an undue risk to the nation's health-care system. Was Thane's venture dangerous? Sure. But that's his problem, he doesn't need to justify taking those risks any more than I need to justify riding silly-fast down some new-to-me backroad. If the rest of the world doesn't like it, they can change the channel, switch the station, turn the page. What Thane partook in was a solo act of stupidity, an individual risk, and I applaud his courage in pursuing something that was important to him. Even if it was really dumb. Or didn't take him through my home town. Speaking of which, the only thing in Thane's letter I would take serious issue with is his suggestion that Moncton, N.B., might possess some redeeming qualities.

Come on, Thane, get real.

Note: Moncton, New Brunswick, Silliker's home town, has suffered the abuse of my jibes for years. Nothing personal, but it would be nice if the locals learned how to drive...
—Max

How stupid of me

May 2002

Forgive me CC readers for I have sinned. I drove a motorhome. While pulling a trailer. With motorcycles in the trailer. To make a long excuse short, it all started with the words "Hey Uncle Max, I got an idea." That's my nephew speaking. He's an ex-football-player nouveau high-roller. And once an idea of his is allowed to roll it's as difficult to stop as an attack of the whim-whams (see below). He praised the benefits of motorhoming—two TVs, satellite connection, VCR, two air-conditioners, two queen-size beds, on-board shower and sink and toilet, complete kitchen including a microwave/convection combo, expandable living room, video camera and monitor subbing for the rearview mirror, and on and on. All

> "Before you criticize and abuse, walk a mile in my shoes"—a fine thought as long as someone else is picking up the tab for the fuel.
> —Max

this towing my 12-ft trailer hauling two bikes (one for the street, one for the dirt). Caught up in his energy of the moment, I lapsed into disgrace, Jackie and I straying from the path of two-wheeled righteousness onto the TrashCanada en route from Ontario to B.C. Having looked at life from both sides now, here's my report from the inside of a 32-ft motor-monster.

Fill 'er up. Way up

First surprise was how easy it is to pilot a boxcar through traffic. Homing along at about 120-130 km/h, we passed all sorts of transport while cursing the moving moto-chicanes that persistently dawdle along just shy of the speed limit. In fact it was in the process of passing a line of fellow motorhomists that I experienced an epiphany: Most motorhomes don't need to crawl along at an annoying and interfering pace. Most possess the motor–such as the Ford V10 in our rig–to easily surpass posted limits. So why do driver/inhabitants insist on impeding world progress?

An initial thought might be to blame fuel consumption. I never worked out the specs for our behemoth except to note that about every 600 km or so my credit card took a $150 hit. To put that in motorcycle touring perspective, Jackie and I could have taken three weeks and ridden the bike to B.C. and back–food, fuel, accommodation and snacks included–for what it cost to feed the motorhome's gas tank. So looking at the big picture (the windshield in this rig is humongous), the ability to cook meals on the go wasn't such a big saving, though the smell of a roasting chicken wafting through the cabin while chasing a sunset in northern Ontario remains a savory memory.

Anyway, it could be argued that such motor-lethargy is born out of a desire to minimize fuel consumption. Certainly less fuel is consumed at lower speeds. But such apparent logic ignores the root cause of the problem. Motorhomes travel slow because–and this was scientifically arrived at following extensive interviews, observation, and research–most of the operators are stupid.

Only the stupid would attempt to justify owning or operating such a societal irritant. So what if we could watch Wile E. Coyote chase the Road Runner as we sped across the prairies, or opt for the antics of Mr. Bean instead of soaking up the majesty of Mt. Robinson? Or have a shower at 130 km/h? Or a pee? Besides treating every gas station as some all-you-can-slurp fossil-fuel buffet, these visual blights of the highway hoard valuable road space. And what of the trail of trash and soiled water it leaves in its toxic wake? Snowmobiles excepted, no other vehicle pollutes more when measured on a distance per person basis. And have you noticed the names given to these brontoslugoruses? Northwind, Softwind, East Breeze, all words that conjure up images that lie about this aerodynamic atrocity. How about Breeze Battle, Air Aggression, or Wham-the-Wind?

Which reminds me, back to the whim-whams (whereby fluids suddenly exit one's body via any convenient orifice, typically at the same time). Jackie and I suffered a 24-hour flu after docking at a friend's B.C. driveway. Here, the motorhome proved a godsend, allowing us to be sick and disgusting in privacy. I renamed our motor-sanitarium Analwind. Once recovered, we set out on the bike to explore mountain trails, leaving nephew to empty diarrheal and vomitus holding tanks.

Rolling rest stop
The other motorhome advantage surfaced on the trip home when a trailer-tire blew in the 40-degree C heat of Saskatchewan. With air-conditioners humming, nephew watched football on TV while I photographed a flattened feline (one more failed reenactment of the famed crossing by the chicken), the rest of the crew sipping cool drinks as we waited three hours for the service truck to arrive. Yep, I had neglected to pack trailer spare, jack, and lug wrench, further proof of the stupidity premise. So motorhomes are good places in which to be sick and/or wait for repairs. Following this deflating incident, the motorhome and bike amicably split, one headed for the TrashCanada, the other in search of empty roads. Even in the heat of the topographically challenged prairies it was grand to be back on the bike. This is not to say that I won't get caught up in another of my nephew's mad schemes, but this much is certain—homes weren't meant to motor.

Running on mountain time

June 2002

Mountains are wondrous spectacles, captivating when viewed from any angle. From above, cruising at an altitude of 30,000 ft (funny how aircraft never cruise in metric), mountains can appear rugged and unpeopled—but wait, that line, there's a road wiggling between snowcaps. Or from a distance, crossing a dry, desert-like expanse of sagebrush, mountains wavering dream-like on the horizon, details lost in a haze of heat—but there, another line, a trail shimmering across a mountain's brown face like a fluid scar. Or from a mountain's base, the assumption of grandeur now startlingly real, expanding ever upward to vanish into wispy clouds—but here, right before me, a raggedy road of washouts and potholes scampering into thick woods, the road's entrance

Sometimes, especially when travelling on a motorcycle, what I see reaches far deeper into my soul than the obvious images presented by my eyes. And the more remote the setting, the farther those images travel beyond my retinas. You see what you want to see, I suppose. So maybe I need new glasses.
  —Max

teasing with hints of unseen twists and switchbacks and panoramas en route to... where? Maybe the road climbs to the top, or spills out onto a valley, or squeezes into whatever narrow passage is left between cliffs and water. You never know until the seduction is over. Damn those mountain roads, I can't seem to leave them alone. Or maybe they can't leave me alone.

House of Windsor
It was a lazy road tucked between mountains, a well-maintained bit of hard-pack, the current tenant of an old railway bed, that brought me to Trout Lake. I had ridden about 400 km to get here, with at least another 100 to go before day's end, much of the ride over scraps of anorexic bush trails starving for traction and choking with dust. So the introduction of pavement is a welcome novelty. It begins just before the village, carrying me through a gridwork of empty streets, the adjacent land mostly unhoused, traces of lumps in uncut grass the only indication buildings ever stood here. Except where the hotel naps.

The Windsor Hotel is an imposing three-storey, wooden structure of white clapboard and forest-green trim capped by a steep, sheet-metal roof of galvanized grey. Sinister clouds of the same hue case the joint from above as I park the bike at the foot of the hotel's facade. Two storeys of veranda face me, full-length steps running along the first level, white railings bordering the second, pots of flowering pinks, reds, and yellows hanging everywhere from overhead beams. I count 18 such pots before I walk under the sign labelled SALOON. Inside, its all dark-brown wood– dark wooden walls, dark wooden chairs, dark wooden tables, dark wooden bar, dark wooden stares from all-day patrons. I sit down and listen to a country tune, followed by Led Zeppelin, emanating from some dark corner. A rumour had whispered the Windsor Hotel serves good pie. The rumour is right.

There's only one gas station between here and forever. Although the BMW R1150GS I'm riding doesn't need fuel, I decide to top-up its humongous tank anyway, simply for the amusement value. I park the Beemer next to the pumps, a pair of hand-operated, gravity feed relics.

These tall, cylindrical, glass-topped antiques stand proud under a carport overhang of white clapboard, the pumps serving passing strangers since before my dad was old enough to buy gas, and we buried him years ago. At least, the pump without the OUT OF ORDER sign is still serving. Other notices, also hand-printed in felt marker, decorate the twin whitewashed posts supporting the overhang. I count three No Credit Cards Accepted Cash Only warm greetings while tanking up the Beemer with two and three-quarter imperial gallons of gas. (These pumps don't cruise in metric either.)

Time warp
The gas station is family run, its current proprietors a young couple recently returned to Trout Lake from Vancouver to take over the reins from an ailing mother. This couple could have been teleported out of my past on a magic carpet of hippie incense and far-outness. He sports a bushy beard, hair down to here, T-shirt and blue jeans; she a tank top, long skirt, sandals, and a wild burst of black hair. I think I remember going to a rock concert with them, back in the early '70s—I had my Lotus 7, remember? That right-hand drive open roadster with no doors, numbers from its racing days still adorning the sparse bodywork? Hey, how come you guys forgot to age? My illusion is trashed by the unsightly stain of a tattoo on her arm. Back in my youth only bikers, cops, and other miscreants abused their skin with tattoos; now it's de rigueur. So maybe it was her mother I went to the concert with.

Exit the Trout Lake time warp to the south and immediately, pavement gives way to chunky gravel, the makings of a scrappy, wildly twisted route that in the space of 30 km swings down into six switchbacks, the scent of tumbling water soaking each turn, crumbling cliffs rising up on my left, disappearing at road's edge on my right, small evergreens grabbing any place they can to grow, blind curves, blind crests, hidden traction, the path so narrow I begin to wonder if there's room for me and an imagined logging truck. Then I begin to wonder if there's even room for the truck. Yet at the moment I can't think of any place I would rather be. Damn these mountain roads.

Benchmark perspective

August 2002

When I take over, it's going to be a different world. For one thing—and this is just between me and you; I don't want this leaked to the press—it will be mandatory for all communities to have at least one small-town-sell-everything-type store, each with a veranda, open at the front but roofed, with two benches. The bench to the left, as viewed while approaching the store's front door, is for the locals. The one to the right is for folks who just happen by. Both benches face out, usually toward the road. Yes, yes, I'll get around to ending all wars, poverty, and famine soon enough, but first things first, eh?

The idea came to me while on tour. I wasn't looking for a veranda protocol as I followed lazy lines of grey pavement through an outcrop

It's small events such as this that add texture and memory to a ride, the type of thing that just doesn't seem to happen as much or as often if you travel by car.
—Brian Bosworth, President and CMO, Twisted Edge Publishing Inc. (publisher of the Destination Highways motorcycle travel guides).

There is no better way to travel than by motorcycle. No other option will get you as far, as fast, while still not removing you from your surroundings. Here, I celebrate the pause in travel, a moment spent between bouts of riding.
—Max

of Maritime agriculture; I was just connecting random village dots on the map in my tankbag. The day was sun-baked and thirsty as I idled down the main street—or was the other street the main one?—looking for the standard-issue country-cute emporium. I needed to feel a cold drink tingling my throat, to taste wetness on my tongue. And there, in rural perfection, down-town Notsurewhere, stood the sole candidate, the village corner store by acclamation. I parked in front, the Triumph Tiger loaded up like a Peruvian pack mule, motorcycle and cargo dusted in that handsome patina of unwashed travel. I removed my insecticidal helmet and stepped up on to the veranda.

Opinions from the bench
The bench on the left bulged to its ends with underactive gentlemen bowling out anti-inflammatory remarks about the weather—she's a fine day was the consensus—and how Judith's eldest son moved to the city and got himself a job (not a good thing, from what I could gather). I set my helmet down on the vacant bench to the right and asked if cold drinks were sold inside. Now, on the surface this might have seemed a dumb question considering the citizens of the bench were all sipping on some sort of soft drink. But it wasn't. In fact it would have been rude not to ask. From the bench I was informed of the store's entire beverage inventory, which ones were the coldest, the oldest stock, Dr. Pepper was the last drink George had before he keeled over with a heart attack (I noticed none of them were drinking George's choice), and so on. Near as I could tell, none of these people worked at the store, they just occupied the bench to the left of the door.

With a thanks I pried away from this soda education long enough to sneak inside through a slam-shut screen door and purchase an orange juice. Returning to the veranda—screen door slamming again—I took my place on the other bench, my hand already dampened by condensation fast gathering on the chilled bottle. Funny how, when you're riding solo, or even when taking your sweetie along, strangers are inclined to talk to the dreaded motorcyclist. Had I been riding with a group, the bench people would likely have kept to themselves in subdued mutter. Now, the conversation started up as soon as I was seated. "Great-looking bike," one of the citizens offered. This is a common opener, even if the general opinion is that the bike is bloody ugly. And no doubt it was discussed in my absence. I nodded, and said something like "Yeah, it does the trick." They asked where I'm from, where I'm headed, how long have I been gone, and how soon do I have to be back home, carefully weighing each answer against bench precedents. We carried on like this for maybe an hour–nobody paid much attention to time–until, with my drink consumed, I announced "Well, I guess I had better hit the road, nice talking to you." They recited the usual meaningless but friendly farewells–ride safely, take care, that sort of chatter–and soon I was back riding, aiming the pack-Tiger out of town down that other road to see which of the two streets was more main.

Veranda please
Just now, as I write this, I realize that, caught up in the pleasures of lazy conversation, I forgot to add the name of the town to my wrinkled touring notes. Doesn't matter, for it's not the town I'm writing about but the veranda. And once my coup de monde is fait accompli (that's in code so the major powers of the world–who seem to have trouble understanding plain English–won't be alerted to my intentions), every village, town, and city will have a corner store. With a veranda. And two benches. Because if it encourages strangers to start talking we won't need to worry about doing anything to end wars, poverty, and famine. It'll just happen. And if that doesn't work, I'll ride back to the Maritimes, track down that misplaced veranda, and all the verandas in between, grab a drink out of the cooler on each occasion, sit down on the bench to the right and talk the problem over with the various citizens of the various benches. I'm sure they'll have an answer. Although, with verandas now in every community, I could be gone for months. Or years. Yes, compulsory verandas is beginning to sound like an even better idea than I first imagined. Prepare for the revolution.

The great unravelling

November/December 2002

Aging sucks. I'm not geriatric—yet—but already the insults of time are dropping by uninvited. Hair regeneration has begun to wane in the vicinity of where evolution intended head-hair to be—my skull's apex. Seems grey hair lacks the energy to get up that high, even though "high" often isn't where it used to be, as I increasingly spend more of my time lying down. Then, a quick glance into the mirror, and what's this shit? Hair growing out of my ears. In half a century I've never managed to own that much fuzz on my face. So this really sucks. More disruptive, however, is the pain, on duty 24 hours no matter what I do, no matter what drugs I take, the dues of past indulgences I suspect, no sympathy requested or required. Yet such afflictions don't amount

Perhaps because motorcycles are not really a rational way to travel, eccentrics seem drawn to these peculiar vehicles. So fortunately we're all in good company and I'm proud to be able to refer to many of these eccentrics as friends. Here's a story about one of them that illustrates why being an eccentric may be the best way to enjoy that fleeting experience called life.
—Max

to much when stacked up against aging's real bummer—friends are beginning to die.

Going, going...
The older we get, the older our friends get, the more likely someone we care about is going to bump off. The latest for me is Luc. I couldn't classify Luc as a close friend, but certainly a good friend. I met him at Peter Hoogeveen's inaugural Blackfly 1600 in nearby North Bay, Ontario. Luc had just beaten cancer and was there to celebrate by riding a minimum of 1,600 km in less than 24 hours. Personally, I think it's nuts to stay up all night dodging deer in the dark when you could be at home sleeping, but as I generally gravitate toward the wacko elements of society, I was on hand to help out. At least between naps. Luc finished the rally in high spirits and we began to correspond. That's when I discovered he was a lawyer working for trade unions, which probably would have ended the friendship right there had I not also heard how he was once reprimanded by a judge for loudly denouncing a corporate lawyer as a "fucking liar." In the courtroom. So he got my respect.

When Luc returned for the second Blackfly, his BMW K1200RS had a new paint job—he had dropped it, his deteriorating muscles unable to halt a slow, parking-lot topple. The bike also sported a higher windshield, this in response to the other new addition, the one for Luc—a small plastic tube sticking out of his trachea. The cancer had returned, his Beemer's new size-large windshield pushing aside wind that might otherwise steal away his breath. Still, Luc remained feisty, his gravelly voice expressing an unconcealed eagerness to do the Blackfly. And to enjoy life. So he rode off into whatever secrets a northern night might choose to reveal in the narrow beam of a motorcycle's headlight and I went to bed, thinking that it takes more guts than I can muster to challenge life with such intensity while staring death in the face. With Luc's bi-annual dose of sleep deprivation behind him, we continued to correspond, discussing replacement bike choices, preferably something with a lower centre of gravity.

The following summer I travelled west to explore traces of old stagecoach routes and abandoned railway lines in the mountains of B.C. En route, southern Alberta, in some blistering hot, windswept side-dish of a town boasting a sorry-looking gas station as its primary industry, I noticed a head poking around the gas pumps. Luc! We immediately embraced, overcome by surprise and the sight of familiar faces caught among blowing sagebrush and cowboy hats. Luc was returning east from the west coast of Canada, alone on a BMW R1200C, a red bandanna wrapped around his trachea tube, arms supported by slings to make hanging on to the handlebars a little easier. Later, this chance meeting made for some fun exchanges, our e-chat tapering off as winter flowed into spring. But that's the way it goes as life perpetually gets in the way of living. A month short of the third Blackfly, a friend of Luc's called to say that he had "passed away." Such an odd term to announce a death. Yet is there any better?

One thread at a time
The fragile fabric of friendship is an intricate weave of countless elements. For example, in my gang's case a general disdain for societal protocol rates highly, ditto a disdain for ill-conceived and blindly enforced laws, and of course a perverse sense of humour is a must. Yet motorcycling is the thread that initially drew us together. All my closest friendships spawned during the last two decades owe their existence to a common interest in motorcycling. And it is those friendships that provide much of the enjoyment I derive out of motorcycling. Which makes it all the more a bitch when a friend checks out. It's as if a piece of the pleasure of motorcycling has been torn away. Kenny, Luc, who's next? As time passes the fabric is only going to get rattier.

Ear hairs I can trim, at least until the curse of vanity collapses into a dumpster of dentures, Depends, and drool, and I no longer give a damn. But there's nothing any of us can do about the eventual loss of friends except to enjoy their company now while we can. So call up an old friend and go for a ride. Age and ear hairs tend to disappear among the ghosts and breezes that dance past a speeding helmet.

Beemer me up

January 2003

This past July, the BMW Motorcycle Owners of America (BMW MOA) chose to hold its annual rally on the dark side of U.S. borders, a first. And BMW MOA being the largest BMW club in the world, wherever it holds its rally a whack of motorcycles is sure to follow. This certainly surprised at least one restaurant in downtown Trenton, Ontario, when thousands of Beemerphiles from all over North America turned up for breakfast on Saturday. But how were Trentonites to know that their town was about to witness the largest Canadian motorcycle rally—and perhaps one-day consumption of coffee, two eggs, toast, and home fries—not held in Port Dover on any given Friday the 13th?

As a gathering of primarily BMW riders, this rally arguably

It's tough for anything in life to get any weirder than a BMW rally. Of course, not many BMW riders enjoy having this pointed out to them, but as the resident expert on weird, and an occasional BMW rider, I felt it was my duty. More than about BMW riders, this column is in praise of weird.
—Max

made for the largest accumulation of eclectic oddballs in Canada. Judged from afar, such as standing atop the berm of the rally site's outdoor amphitheatre, it would seem to be a homogeneous sea of Teutonic motorcycles, white T-shirts, and grey hair. But wade in and, jeez, will you look at all the sidecars. Beemerists seem to like sidecars, ones that lean, ones that remain vertical while the bike leans, two-seaters, hardtops, no tops, basically every variety known to hackos; odd considering that BMWs handle quite well on their own two wheels.

And check out the yards and metres of colourful Gortex being traipsed about. Sadly, Gortex and its imitators rarely match leather's ability to highlight a female form. However, as most of the good-looking women were closer to my age than the average porn star—kids and grandchildren thankfully left home in Nebraska or wherever—the triumph of comfort over style was understandable. And certainly more sensible than the many shorts-and-T-shirt riding outfits, blazing heat notwithstanding. Lots of open-face helmets in attendance too (though I saw no tiny-Tupperware yarmulkes) which might lead one to suspect that BMWists are keen to protect their brains, but don't think much of their faces. And before we leave the fashion report, how about the fluorescent school-crossing-guard vests? Seems a quarter of all Beemerites are either safety zealots or potential pedophiles.

Adventures in luggage

No BMW model was missing from this moto-smorgasbord—luxo-tourers, ergonomically-challenged sportbikes, sport-tourers, vintage boxers chugging about, one or two old singles, plenty of newer 650 singles, and a personal fave, the air-cooled boxer-twin GS decked out in that trendy adventure-touring look. A properly experienced GS bike comes cloaked in a seasoned film of bugs and Alaska dirt, at least that portion of the bike visible beneath the obligatory mounds of luggage. BMW factory luggage is nowhere, man; the hindquarters of any genuine nomadic GS is burdened down with humongous metal containers—recycled steamer trunks or possibly waste disposal dumpsters stolen from some urban back alley—the boxes wallpapered in hundreds of smudged stickers of remote and far-away places (assuming the bike is remote and far away from those places at the time of viewing).

Piled above these containers are any or all of a tent, camping stove, axe, maybe an inflatable raft, plus five or six pickup loads of other necessities, occasionally topped off with a teetering cage restraining some yappy little hound only its owner wouldn't think to strap under the wheel of a transport truck. To the front of the heavily padded seat sits a tankbag large enough to hold the total gear of a hockey team, sticks included. Bulging fabric panniers are making a comeback, though on one particularly overloaded cargocycle, two ungainly misshapen boxes stretched forward out beyond the fuel tank, twin army-surplus bazooka cases, I think, each with enough room for gun and a war's worth of accompanying ammo.

Been there, carried that
High above this clutter stands the rider, for they don't ever seem to ride sitting down, even when crossing the flat, smooth, paved surface of a parking lot. (So why the padded seat?) The captain at the bridge usually sports one of those front-end-loader style full-face helmets, raised open to display a week's worth of facial stubble (regardless of gender), the image not so much Miami-vice as Miami-wino, the rider draped in muddied and weathered Aerostich, tall and unwashed, a perfect match for the bike.

Typically, the pirate ship and its treasure weave through the lesser craft, stirring a wake of admiring glances while searching for that one special campsite only a veteran traveller could find in such close proximity to the beer tent. Much more than a rat bike, this is a pack-rat bike. Been there and back, and managed to cart everything along. Except soap.

I revel in rallies like this, ones crammed to the fences with serious nutcases who offer a smile of understanding when you make eye-contact rather than a puzzled stare, or worse, a glare that warns they want to beat you up. So the BMW MOA can rally here in Canada any time it likes. Just check the dog cages at the border with the bazookas, okay?

Who's the poseur?

April 2003

Much has been made of the weekend badass-biker look, where "professionals" dress up like nasty bikers and then bike-belch about the neighbourhood, exhausting in obnoxiously loud tones to ensure maximum attention. Typically, these off-duty professionals exchange the conservative appearance and demeanour demanded by day-to-day lives to take on the persona exemplified by the biker outfit. Rich Urban Biker, or rubbies, the press labelled them as the pretend baddies learned to walk that walk and curse that talk. Yes, we mocked, even called them poseurs, but–annoying exhausts aside–where's the harm?

My wife makes dance costumes for kids. To witness the joy a small child experiences after donning a

There's nothing wrong with reality that a good fantasy can't cure. Believe me, I know.
–Max

new costume is a genuine treat. Suddenly, a child among children becomes a princess or prince or whatever other persona suggested by the outfit. It is a treasured moment of escape, an all-too-infrequent opportunity to become special in one's own eyes—eyes radiating with pleasure and dreams and imagination. And to varying degrees, a costume works that same magic on the child in all of us. Where would Cinderella have been without a fancy dress and glass slippers? Still scouring floors no doubt, which is likely where she ended up anyway after marrying that chauvinist prince. But for that one brief evening of ecstasy, she bathed in the excitement of her costume.

Card tricks

Fairy godmothers wielding magic wands are pure fantasy of course. In the reality of the 21st century we use credit cards to do the same trick. So with the flick of a wafer of plastic, Randy real-estate agent becomes weekend badass biker in black leather, chaps, buckles, and fringes. And fingerless gloves. And a helmet the likes of which his mother might have served out a bowl of soup. Campbell's Cream of Noodlehead. Just be back at your desk at Pumpkin International Inc. first thing Monday morning, poseur.

Yet Randy is not alone in buying into a fantasy. Look, there's Avery accountant as snazzy sport-bike rider, looking fast and dapper-dandy in leathers colour-matched to the bike, ditto the dainty boots, palm-studded gloves, and famous-racer-signature helmet. And over there, two escapees masquerading as a touring couple, both parties to the charade resplendently decked out in identical outfits, with names embroidered on a breast pocket—Stan, Mildred—and maybe their home town—Bancroft, Ontario, Canada—across the costume's back. Or maybe Mr. (or Ms.) Dress-Up is a dirt rider this weekend, bearing the blight of eye-sore dayglo into the forest. And likely a haze of two-stroke defoliant too. Or perhaps it's the costume of the non-conformist on display, which is to appear as if you, the individual, don't give a rat's buttock about appearances. (On a personal note, I find dirty, sun-bleached Gortex ideal for this.) Did I miss anyone? Doesn't matter. The important question is, did you spot the real poseurs?

Look in a mirror, for we are all poseurs. Or we all aren't. To own a motorcycle, or even simply ride one, makes you a "real" motorcyclist. The manner in which you use that motorcycle, how often, where, and number of kilometres is your choice, as is the related costume. Truth is, no human is immune to the effect of costume. And with one general exception, this is a good thing. It's an easy, harmless escape as all that ails us gets left behind in the over-crowded closet of responsibility. So let the rubbies roll on—preferably with a cork jammed up the exhaust—and rejoice that we can so easily exercise our right to escape.

Uniform difference
So what's that general exception? When costume transforms into uniform. This can happen by requirement of association—such as with biker gangs, cops and the military—or simply by coincidental association—such as when a bunch of people of like appearance end up in the same spot. Bureaucrats schmoozing on parliament hill for instance, or perhaps a gathering of motorcyclists at a Sunday-morning breakfast stop. Whatever the situation, the strength of a costume's persona grows exponentially as numbers of the similarly dressed increase. The individual's fantasy melds into the group, for it's not simply the clothing that becomes uniform but also thought. Put on a uniform and assume the associated head space, invariably one of group strength and power, the role of the individual subjugated to the objectives of the group as escapee becomes captive. So much power in a simple set of clothes.

As with everything in life, costumes have a good side and a bad side. But the risk of costume converting to uniform should not deter anyone from entertaining the child within by partaking in an innocent fantasy. Unless you're a convicted mass-murderer or similar scoundrel, escape is good. Although, come to think of it, perhaps we could all steal a page from the incarcerated by keeping the noise down during the escape. In other words, would all you poseurs please put a gag on those loud pipes? Nice outfit, though.

Safe underwear at any speed

June 2003

The dictionary definition of "safety" can encompass motorcycle helmets, but I don't buy it. Helmets, seat belts and related "safety equipment" have little to do with safety. Instead, these are things to wear in the event of an accident. Like clean underwear. Such equipment merely mitigates damage (or embarrassment) once an accident happens. And we as a society find it much easier to mitigate damage than to avoid damage, concentrating our resources on mandating or cajoling citizens into donning all sorts of weird paraphernalia that might help compensate for our collective inabilities to do things right–such as ride a motorcycle.

Humans have always pushed the limits of safety. Studies have documented our unconscious keenness

Humanity is so easily conned, particularly when the acting con artist (elected or otherwise) associates the pitch with sacred motherhood issues, such as freedom, democracy, security, peace and safety. But when you get right down to it, it's all a crock of shit. And not even a safe and secure one. This column merely exposes the slippery tip of the iceberg.
–Max

to take two steps into danger for every single step made in the name of safety. I'm a fan of anti-lock brakes (ABS). Yet when first introduced in cars, one study among German taxi drivers found that those who were told their taxis had ABS invariably began following much closer to the car in front than when in the same model of car devoid of ABS–much closer even than the supposed safety advantage would theoretically have allowed. So we're not too bright that way. But imagine the inverse. Take the average SUV owner out of the "safety" cocoon of airbags and miles of metal and stick them into an open-air vehicle of fragile frame, helmets and seat belts and air-bags replaced by a mere wisp of polluted air hanging between them and surrounding transports. What are the odds these ex-SUVers would be as inclined to cellphone distraction while playing the vehicular equivalent of "now-I've-got-you-you-son-of-a-bitch," blocking others attempts to merge into "their" lane, tailgating, daydreaming of office paramours, and similar vehicular hijinks?

Not my fault
Obviously it's much easier to travel in an air-bagged, armour-plated SUV than to learn how to drive. And that's the problem with this current obsession with safety–all these mandatory gizmos encourage us to ignore safe practices, choosing instead to place our lives in the hands of technology. Our safety is no longer our problem and failure is never our fault. The basic premise is that any idiot should be able to schmuck anything into anything and survive, and should any injury result, the machine's manufacturer should be held at fault rather than the machine's operator. Politicians know that demanding road-competence from voters would downgrade at least half the population to bus travel. But look at the positive side–this could be a real boost to ridership on public transit. The preferable political route is to simply obscure truth behind tired clich s, authorities given to spewing out such dandies as "A driver's license is not a right; it's a privilege." So if a license is not a right, why are the roads increasingly burdened by incompetents? Face it, if you fail to get a driver's licence in Canada, likely you aren't even up to operating a grocery cart. The only reason we haven't witnessed huge increases in traffic deaths is that, thanks to Nader-think, we have surrounded the incompetent in "safety equipment." So our roads have become a carnival for bumper

cars, the larger the vehicle the better (read "safer"); who cares about the damage inflicted on anyone who dares get in the way of incompetence?

Knock on wood
But hey, accidents happen eh? Bullshit. More likely, stupidity happens. Have you heard that oft-voiced excuse for incompetence among motorcyclists? "There are two kinds of riders—those who have had an accident, and those who will." So what kind of moron starts out on a ride assuming a crash is inevitable? Or with that accident behind them, all is well? Hasn't anyone thought about avoiding a crash? And does this column have too many questions?

No question, during my 30-plus years of motorcycling, much of the Canadian terrain has become permanently marred from my off-road antics. But I've yet to crash a bike while street riding. Hundreds of thousands of kilometres, much of it at silly speeds while skimming across the edges of questionable surfaces, and no hits. Still, I never ride without helmet and piles of protective clothing. I don't give a damn whether it's the law or not, I wear this stuff because I like to push limits and recognize that one day I might screw up. And because I rely strictly on me for my safety—not protective equipment, or you, or road conditions—so far I haven't needed the stuff. The equipment is only there to lessen the damage in the unlikely event of a crash (or fleeting moment of stupidity).

If society is seriously concerned about preventing traffic-related deaths and injury, isn't it better to insist on competent vehicle operators than to pile on protective gear upon protective gear and then send out the forces to punish those who fail to wear mittens when headed out into the cold? What's next, roadside checks for clean underwear? Real safety comes from operator skill and intelligent judgement, not legislated reliance on protective equipment.

Sidecar à la carte

August 2003

Perhaps it was the heat of the sun blazing out of a cloudless sky, or the sweet scent of Castrol R choking the air, or the noxious plumes of assorted two-stroke toxins drifting about, or a mixture of everything, I don't know, but last August during the VRRA's Vintage Festival at Mosport, while wandering around the paddock, I bought a sidecar. No bike with it, just a Velorex sidecar boasting a few cracks and dents and a For Sale sign. No obvious way to get it home. Not even enough money with me to buy it. But thanks to a trusting owner and a racer friend with an enclosed trailer (borrowed, mind you), next day the Velorex arrived at my barn door.

First thing I did was set it up on blocks and start doing an inventory of bits. What's this? Looks like

An affair with motorcycles can take you down many very different roads, on many very different bikes. And sometimes, the road can run slightly askew of motorcycling. Just part of the wonder of it all.
—Max

a convertible top, brand new. And there's a windshield, the Perspex still covered in its vinyl protective sheeting, never used. I installed the windshield, erected the top, and then ran up to the house to get Jackie. She had to see this—it was just so ugly it was beautiful. And laughable. I was in love. Then I realized I would probably need a motorcycle for it.

Cart before the horse
I know, I know, should have thought of that before. No excuses, as it certainly wasn't my first experience with sidecars. Years ago, Jackie and I rode around Brazil in an Amazonas sidecar rig and had a blast. And not quite as long ago we hacked around Washington state in a Ural rig, again enjoying ourselves immensely. So I knew I would need a bike. And I also knew what fun a sidecar could be. Not that it can compete with the joys of an unattached motorcycle, for when a bike is wed to sidecar it basically ruins the motorcycle experience. What you get instead is a whole new experience—not a motorcycle, not a car, but definitely a giggle. So the idea of getting one has bumped around in my head for most of those same many years.

On one occasion a rider turned up at the Sportbike Rally in Parry Sound with a sidecar rig, rode in, and in not much more time than it takes to tell about it, rode out again without the sidecar, and I thought, that's the way to do it. Stick the car on in a minute or so, then detach it with equal expediency when you want a real bike. Best of both worlds. And those two worlds can be had for very little extra cash and no added insurance costs. So with the idea of a sidecar well-planted, all I needed was the steeped fumes of old motorcycles to cause it to gel into that thick goo of motivation.

As for a suitable motorcycle to match, sticking one of these things onto a bike lacking a traditional cradle frame—metal tubing running around and under the engine, connecting to the upper part of the frame front and back—can be an engineering nightmare (true, engineers likely invented the nightmare, but that's another story). So that ruled out most of the bikes on my fave list. Except Suzuki's Bandit, either in 1200 or 600 configurations. Coincidentally, about a month before my impromptu sidecar acquisition, I had swapped bikes with friend and former CC-staffer Larry Tate, he riding my BMW F650GS, me on his Bandit 1200. Although the ride was brief, it wasn't slow, the Bandit proving to be smooth and comfortable, with reasonably good handling.

And it had the right frame. And by current pricing, the Bandit's a genuine bargain.

But, as you may have gathered from the above tale, I tend to move quickly only on a motorcycle. Have to think about things, consider all my options, wait for the wind to change, find the courage to open a wallet, and other delays. It was during such heady contemplation that I happened upon a one-owner, low-mileage, Yamaha Seca XJ650. This is a bike I lusted after when it was introduced to Canada over 20 years ago, and one that possesses a proper frame and shaftdrive to boot. And it was an even better bargain than the Bandit. So I bought it.

Age before beauty
One of the nice things about an older-but-not-yet-antique bike is that, suddenly, duct tape is okay again. And if the bike needs to be modified to suit your needs, Vise-Grip mindset will do. There's no peer pressure to buy the latest tricknology, because there isn't any to buy. Cobble, twist, tape, and ride. And I had forgotten what a joy this bike is to ride. It's a bike that shines when ridden down a twisty road, or a highway, fast, slow, one-up, two-up. Even unwashed. Sure, the front brakes were a bit of a fright as I rode it home, but the more I squeezed on the lever, the less wooden the brakes felt, leaving me to think that the previous owner likely refrained from using that dangerous part of the motorcycle. And while the bike's outer bits are scratched and a little worn, its heart and soul still beat strong, as if thrilled to be released to run the backroads–whoa, there's another, wooden brake, on the throttle, to hell with age. In fact, the little Seca's been so much fun to ride that I have yet to hook up the sidecar. But I'll get around to it. Maybe some day in August with the sun blazing out of a cloudless sky because–as I mentioned–I tend to move fast only on a motorcycle.

Around the Bend (again) and *On Any Wednesday (Or Tuesday, or Thursday, or...)* can be purchased through any quality bookstore. For a list of dealers stocking these books please contact the publisher. To purchase directly from the publisher, complete the order form below and forward cheque or money order to the publisher. Thank you for your interest in Word Dust Press.
(For telephone or credit card orders: 1-888-229-2665)

ORDER FORM

Name _____

Address _____

Apt#, RR#, etc _____

City _____ Prov/State _____

PC/Zip _____ Country _____

phone _____ e-mail (optional) _____

Please send me:
____ copies *On Any Wednesday*
____ copies *Around the Bend (again)*
at $18.69 each: $ _____
plus shipping & handling:
($5.00 first book, $2.00 for each additional book) $ _____
                                          Subtotal $ _____

GST/HST on subtotal (R126471259):
Residents of Newfoundland and Labrador,
New Brunswick, and Nova Scotia add 15% HST: $ _____
All other Canadian residents, add 7% GST: $ _____
                                        Total $ _____

☐ Yes, please have the author sign my copies.

Requested salutation _____

☐ Add me to your mailing list.

Word Dust Press, RR1, 693 Groulx Rd.,
Astorville, ON P0H 1B0

E-mail: books@worddust.ca
Web site: http://www.worddust.ca